English Men of Letters

EDITED BY JOHN MORLEY

DRYDEN

DRYDEN

BY

G. SAINTSBURY

AMS PRESS
NEW YORK

Reprinted from the edition of 1888, London
First AMS EDITION published 1968
Manufactured in the United States of America

Library of Congress Catalogue Card Number: 68-58394

AMS PRESS, INC.
New York, N.Y. 10003

PREFATORY NOTE.

A WRITER on Dryden is more especially bound to acknowledge his indebtedness to his predecessors, because,
so far as matters of fact are concerned, that indebtedness
must necessarily be greater than in most other cases.
There is now little chance of fresh information being
obtained about the poet, unless it be in a few letters
hitherto undiscovered or withheld from publication. I
have therefore to acknowledge my debt to Johnson,
Malone, Scott, Mitford, Bell, Christie, the Rev. R.
Hooper, and the writer of an article in the *Quarterly
Review* for 1878. Murray's " Guide to Northamptonshire " has been of much use to me in the visits I have
made to Dryden's birthplace, and the numerous other
places associated with his memory in his native county.
To Mr. J. Churton Collins I owe thanks for pointing
out to me a Dryden house which, so far as he and I
know, has escaped the notice of previous biographers.
Mr. W. Noel Sainsbury, of the Record Office, has supplied
me with some valuable information. My friend Mr.
Edmund W. Gosse has not only read the proof-sheets of
this book with the greatest care, suggesting many things
of value, but has also kindly allowed me the use of original
editions of many late seventeenth-century works, including

most of the rare pamphlets against the poet in reply to his satires.

Except Scott's excellent but costly and bulky edition, there is, to the disgrace of English booksellers or book-buyers, no complete edition of Dryden. The first issue of this in 1808 was reproduced in 1821 with no material alterations, but both are very expensive, especially the second. A tolerably complete and not unsatisfactory Dryden may however be got together without much outlay by any one who waits till he can pick up at the bookshops copies of Malone's edition of the prose works, and of Congreve's original edition (duodecimo or folio) of the plays. By adding to these Mr. Christie's admirable Globe edition of the poems, very little, except the translations, will be left out, and not too much obtained in duplicate. This, of course, deprives the reader of Scott's life and notes, which are very valuable. The life, however, has been reprinted, and is easily accessible.

In the following pages a few passages from a course of lectures on "Dryden and his Period," delivered by me at the Royal Institution in the spring of 1880, have been incorporated.

CONTENTS.

DRYDEN.

CHAPTER I.

BEFORE THE RESTORATION.

JOHN DRYDEN was born on the 9th of August, 1631, at the Vicarage of Aldwinkle All Saints, between Thrapston and Oundle. Like other small Northamptonshire villages Aldwinkle is divided into two parishes, All Saints and St. Peter's, the churches and parsonage-houses being within bowshot of each other, and some little confusion has arisen from this. It has, however, been cleared up by the industrious researches of various persons, and there is now no doubt about the facts. The house in which the poet was born (and which still exists, though altered to some extent internally) belonged at the time to his maternal grandfather, the Rev. Henry Pickering. The Drydens and the Pickerings were both families of some distinction in the county, and both of decided Puritan principles ; but they were not, properly speaking, neighbours. The Drydens originally came from the neighbourhood of the border, and a certain John Dryden, about the middle of the sixteenth century, married the daughter and heiress of Sir John Cope, of Canons Ashby, in the county of Northampton. Erasmus, the son of this John Dryden—the name is spelt as usual at the time in half-a-dozen different ways, and there is no reason for supposing that the poet invented the *y*, though before him it seems to have been usually Driden—was created a baronet, and his third son, also an Erasmus, was the poet's father. Before this Erasmus married Mary Pickering the families had already been connected, but they lived on opposite sides of the county, Canons Ashby being in the hilly district which extends to the borders of Oxfordshire on the south-west, while Tichmarsh, the headquarters of the Pickerings, lies on the extreme east on high ground, overlooking the flats of Huntingdon. The poet's father is described as " of Tichmarsh," and seems to have usually resided in that neighbourhood. His property, however, which descended to our poet, lay in the neighbourhood of Canons Ashby at the village of Blakesley, which is not, as the biographers persistently repeat after one another, " near Tichmarsh," but some forty miles distant to the straightest flying crow. Indeed the connexion of the poet with the seat of his ancestors, and of his own property, appears to have been very slight. There is no positive evidence that he was ever at Canons Ashby at all, and this is a pity. For the house—still in the possession of his collateral descendants in the female line—is a very delightful one, looking like a miniature college quadrangle set down by the side of a country lane, with a background of park in which the deer wander, and a fringe of formal garden, full of the trimmest of yew-trees. All this was there in Dryden's youth, and, moreover, the place was the scene of some stirring events. Sir John Driden was a staunch parliamentarian, and his house lay obnoxious to the royalist garrisons of Towcester on the one side, and Ban-

bury on the other. On at least one occasion a great fight
took place, the parliamentarians barricading themselves in
the church of Canons Ashby, within stone's throw of the
house, and defending it and its tower for several hours
before the royalists forced the place and carried them off
prisoners. This was in Dryden's thirteenth year, and a boy
of thirteen would have rejoiced not a little in such a state
of things.

But, as has been said, the actual associations of the
poet lie elsewhere. They are all collected in the valley of
the Nene, and a well-girt man can survey the whole in a
day's walk. It is remarkable that Dryden's name is connected with fewer places than is the case with almost
any other English poet, except, perhaps, Cowper. If we
leave out of sight a few visits to his father-in-law's seat
at Charlton, in Wiltshire, and elsewhere, London and
twenty miles of the Nene valley exhaust the list of
his residences. This valley is not an inappropriate
locale for the poet who in his faults, as well as his
merits, was perhaps the most English of all English
writers. It is not grand, or epic, or tragical, but on the
other hand it is sufficiently varied, free from the monotony of the adjacent fens, and full of historical and architectural memories. The river in which Dryden acquired,
beyond doubt, that love of fishing which is his only trait in
the sporting way known to us, is always present in long
slow reaches, thick with water plants. The remnants of
the great woods which once made Northamptonshire the
rival of Nottingham and Hampshire are close at hand,
and luckily the ironstone workings which have recently
added to the wealth, and detracted from the beauty of the
central district of the county, have not yet invaded
Dryden's region. Tichmarsh and Aldwinkle, the places

of his birth and education, lie on opposite sides of the
river, about two miles from Thrapston. Aldwinkle is
sheltered and low, and looks across to the rising ground
on the summit of which Tichmarsh church rises, flanked
hard by with a huge cedar-tree on the rectory lawn, a
cedar-tree certainly coeval with Dryden, since it was
planted two years before his birth. A little beyond Aldwinkle, following the course of the river, is the small
church of Pilton, where Erasmus Dryden and Mary
Pickering were married on October 21, 1630. All these
villages are embowered in trees of all kinds, elms and
walnuts especially, and the river banks slope in places
with a pleasant abruptness, giving good views of the
magnificent woods of Lilford, which, however, are new
comers comparatively speaking. Another mile or two
beyond Pilton brings the walker to Oundle, which has
some traditional claim to the credit of teaching Dryden
his earliest humanities, and the same distance beyond
Oundle is Cotterstock, where a house, still standing, but
altered, was the poet's favourite sojourn in his later years.
Long stretches of meadows lead thence across the river
into Huntingdonshire, and there, just short of the great
north road, lies the village of Chesterton, the residence, in
the late days of the seventeenth century, of Dryden's
favourite cousins, and frequently his own. All these
places are intimately connected with his memory, and the
last named is not more than twenty miles from the first.
Between Cotterstock and Chesterton, where lay the two
houses of his kinsfolk which we know him to have most
frequented, lies, as it lay then, the grim and shapeless
mound studded with ancient thorn-trees, and looking
down upon the silent Nene, which is all that remains of the
castle of Fotheringhay. Now, as then, the great lantern

of the church, with its flying buttresses and tormented
tracery, looks out over the valley. There is no allusion
that I know of to Fotheringhay in Dryden's works, and,
indeed, there seems to have been a very natural feeling
among all seventeenth century writers on the court side
that the less said about Mary Stuart the better. Fotheringhay waits until Mr. Swinburne shall complete the
trilogy begun in *Chastelard* and continued in *Bothwell*,
for an English dramatic poet to tread worthily in the
steps of Montchrestien, of Vondel, and of Schiller. But
Dryden must have passed it constantly, when he was at
Cotterstock he must have had it almost under his eyes, and
we know that he was always brooding over fit historical
subjects in English history for the higher poetry. Nor is
it, I think, an unpardonable conceit to note the dominance
in the haunts of this intellectually greatest among the par-
tisans of the Stuarts, of the scene of the greatest tragedy,
save one, that befell even that house of the furies.

There is exceedingly little information obtainable about
Dryden's youth. The inscription in Tichmarsh Church,
the work of his cousin Mrs. Creed, an excellent person
whose needle and pencil decorated half the churches and
half the manor-houses in that part of the country, boasts
that he had his early education in that village, while
Oundle, as has been said, has some traditional claims to a
similar distinction. From the date of his birth to his
entry at Westminster School we have no positive information whatever about him, and even the precise date of the
latter is unknown. He was a king's scholar, and it seems
that the redoubtable Busby took pains with him—doubtless in the well-known Busbeian manner—and liked his
verse translations. From Westminster he went to Cambridge, where he was entered at Trinity on May 18th,

1650, matriculated on July 16th, and on October 2nd
was elected to a Westminster scholarship. He was then
nineteen, an instance, be it observed, among many, of the
complete mistake of supposing that very early entrance
into the universities was the rule before our own days. Of
Dryden's Cambridge sojourn we know little more than of
his sojourn at Westminster. He was in trouble on July
19th, 1652, when he was discommonsed and gated for a
fortnight for disobedience and contumacy. Shadwell also
says that while at Cambridge he " scurrilously traduced a
nobleman" and was "rebuked on the head" therefor.
But Shadwell's unsupported assertions about Dryden are
unworthy of the slightest credence. He took his degree
in 1654, and though he gained no fellowship, seems to
have resided for nearly seven years at the university.
There has been a good deal of controversy about the feelings with which Dryden regarded his *alma mater*. It is
certainly curious that, except a formal acknowledgment of
having received his education from Trinity, there is to be
found in his works no kind of affectionate reference to
Cambridge, while there is to be found an extremely unkind
reference to her in his very best manner. In one of his
numerous prologues to the University of Oxford—the
Univerity of Cambridge seems to have given him no occasion of writing a prologue—occur the famous lines—

> Oxford to him a dearer name shall be
> Than his own mother university;
> Thebes did his green unknowing youth engage,
> He chooses Athens in his riper age.

It has been sought to diminish the force of this very left-
handed compliment to Cambridge by quoting a phrase of
Dryden's concerning the " gross flattery that universities

will endure." But I am inclined to think that most university men will agree with me that this is probably a unique instance of a member of the one university going out of his way to flatter the other at the expense of his own. Dryden was one of the most accomplished flatterers that ever lived, and certainly had no need save of delibe-rate choice to resort to the vulgar expedient of insulting one person or body by way of praising another. What his cause of dissatisfaction was it is impossible to say, but the trivial occurrence already mentioned certainly will not account for it.

If, however, during these years we have little testimony about Dryden, we have three documents from his own hand, which are of no little interest. Although Dryden was one of the most late-writing of English poets, he had got into print before he left Westminster. A promising pupil of that school, Lord Hastings, had died of small-pox, and according to the fashion of the time a *tombeau*, as it would have been called in France, was published, contain-ing elegies by a very large number of authors, ranging from Westminster boys to the already famous names of Waller and Denham. Somewhat later an epistle commendatory was contributed by Dryden to a volume of religious verse by his friend John Hoddesdon. Later still, and probably after he had taken his degree, he wrote a letter to his cousin, Honor Driden, daughter of the reigning baronet of Canons Ashby, which the young lady had the grace to keep. All these juvenile productions have been very severely judged. As to the poems, the latest writer on the subject, a writer in the *Quarterly Review*, whom I cer-tainly do not name otherwise than *honoris causâ*, pro-nounces the one execrable, and the other inferior to the juvenile productions of that miserable poetaster, Kirke

White. It seems to this reviewer that Dryden had at
this time " no ear for verse, no command of poetic diction,
no sense of poetic taste." As to the letter, even Scott
describes it as " alternately coarse and pedantic." I am
in hopeless discord with these authorities, both of whom
I respect. Certainly neither the elegy on Lord Hastings,
nor the complimentary poem to Hoddesdon, nor the letter
to Honor Driden, is a masterpiece. But all three show,
as it seems to me, a considerable literary faculty, a remarkable feeling after poetic style, and above all the peculiar
virtue which was to be Dryden's own. They are all
saturated with conceits, and the conceit was the reigning
delicacy of the time. Now if there is one thing more
characteristic and more honourably characteristic of Dryden than another, it is that he was emphatically of his
time. No one ever adopted more thoroughly and more
unconsciously the motto as to *Spartam nactus es.* He tried
every fashion, and where the fashion was capable of being
brought *sub specie æternitatis* he never failed so to bring
it. Where it was not so capable he never failed to abandon
it and to substitute something better. A man of this temperament (which it may be observed is a mingling of the
critical and the poetical temperaments) is not likely to find
his way early or to find it at all without a good many
preliminary wanderings. But the two poems so severely
condemned, though they are certainly not good poems, are
beyond all doubt possessed of the elements of goodness.
I doubt myself whether any one can fairly judge them
who has not passed through a novitiate of careful study of
the minor poets of his own day. By doing this one
acquires a certain faculty of distinguishing, as Théophile
Gautier once put it in his own case, " the sheep of Hugo
from the goats of Scribe." I do not hesitate to say that

an intelligent reviewer in the year 1650 would have ranked Dryden, though perhaps with some misgivings, among the sheep. The faults are simply an exaggeration of the prevailing style, the merits are different.

As for the epistle to Honor Driden, Scott must surely have been thinking of the evil counsellors who wished him to bowdlerise glorious John, when he called it "coarse." There is nothing in it but the outspoken gallantry of an age which was not afraid of speaking out, and the prose style is already of no inconsiderable merit. It should be observed, however, that a most unsubstantial romance has been built up on this letter, and that Miss Honor's father, Sir John Driden, has had all sorts of anathemas launched at him, in the Locksley Hall style, for damming the course of true love. There is no evidence whatever to prove this crime against Sir John. It is in the nature of mankind almost invariably to fall in love with its cousins, and—fortunately according to some physiologists—by no means invariably to marry them. That Dryden seriously aspired to his cousin's hand there is no proof, and none that her father refused to sanction the marriage. On the contrary, his foes accuse him of being a dreadful flirt, and of making "the young blushing virgins die" for him in a miscellaneous but probably harmless manner. All that is positively known on the subject is that Honor never married, that the cousins were on excellent terms some half-century after this fervent epistle, and that Miss Driden is said to have treasured the letter and shown it with pride, which is much more reconcilable with the idea of a harmless flirtation than of a great passion tragically cut short.

At the time of the writing of this epistle Dryden was indeed not exactly an eligible suitor. His father had just died—1654—and had left him two-thirds of the Blakesley estates, with a reversion to the other third at the death of his mother. The land extended to a couple of hundred acres or thereabouts, and the rent, which with characteristic generosity Dryden never increased, though rents went up in his time enormously, amounted to 60*l.* a year. Dryden's two-thirds were estimated by Malone at the end of the last century to be worth about 120*l.* income of that day, and this certainly equals at least 200*l.* to-day. With this to fall back upon, and with the influence of the Driden and Pickering families, any bachelor in those days might be considered provided with prospects, but exacting parents might consider the total inadequate to the support of a wife and family. Sir John Driden is said, though a fanatical Puritan, to have been a man of no very strong intellect, and he certainly did not feather his nest in the way which was open to any defender of the liberties of the people. Sir Gilbert Pickering, who in consequence of the intermarriages before alluded to was doubly Dryden's cousin, was wiser in his generation. He was one of the few members of the Long Parliament who judiciously attached themselves to the fortunes of Cromwell, and was plentifully rewarded with fines, booty, places, and honours, by the Protector. When Dryden finally left Cambridge in 1657 he is said to have attached himself to this kinsman. And at the end of the next year he wrote his remarkable Heroic Stanzas on Cromwell's death. This poem must have at once put out of doubt his literary merits. There was assuredly no English poet then living, except Milton and Cowley, who could possibly have written it, and it was sufficiently different from the style of either of those masters. Taking the four-line stanza, which Davenant had made popular, the poet starts with a

bold opening, in which the stately march of the verse is
not to be disguised by all the frippery of erudition which
loads it :—

> And now 'tis time ; for their officious haste,
>   Who would before have borne him to the sky,
> Like eager Romans, ere all rites were past,
>   Did let too soon the sacred eagle fly.

The whole poem contains but thirty-seven of these
stanzas, but it is full of admirable lines and thoughts. No
doubt there are plenty of conceits as well, and Dryden
would not have been Dryden if there had not been.   But
at the same time the singular justness which always
marked his praise, as well as his blame, is as remarkable
in the matter of the poem, as the force and vigour of the
diction and versification are in its manner.   To this day
no better eulogy of the Protector has been written, and
the poet with a remarkable dexterity evades, without
directly denying, the more awkward points in his hero's
career and character.   One thing which must strike all
careful readers of the poem is the entire absence of any
attack on the royalist party.   To attempt, as Shadwell
and other libellers attempted a quarter of a century later,
to construe a famous couplet—

> He fought to end our fighting, and essayed
> To staunch the blood by breathing of the vein—

into an approval of the execution of Charles I., is to wrest
the sense of the original hopelessly and unpardonably.
Cromwell's conduct is contrasted with that of those who
" the quarrel loved, but did the cause abhor," who " first
sought to inflame the parties, then to poise," &c., i.e. with
Essex, Manchester, and their likes ; and it need hardly be

said that this contrast was ended years before there was
any question of the king's death.   Indeed, to a careful
reader nowadays the Heroic Stanzas read much more
like an elaborate attempt to hedge between the parties
than like an attempt to gain favour from the roundheads
by uncompromising advocacy of their cause.   The author
is one of those " sticklers of the war " that he himself
describes.

It is possible that a certain half-heartedness may have
been observed in Dryden by those of his cousin's party.   It
is possible, too, that Sir Gilbert Pickering, like Thackeray's
Mr. Scully, was a good deal more bent on making use of
his young kinsman than on rewarding him in any perma-
nent manner.   At any rate, no kind of preferment fell to
his lot, and the anarchy of the "foolish Ishbosheth " soon
made any such preferment extremely improbable.   Before
long it would appear that Dryden had definitely given up
whatever position he held in Sir Gilbert Pickering's household, and had betaken himself to literature.   The fact of his
so betaking himself almost implied adherence to the royalist party.   In the later years of the commonwealth, English letters had rallied to a certain extent from the disarray
into which they were thrown by the civil war, but the
centres of the rally belonged almost exclusively to the
royalist party.   Milton had long forsworn pure literature,
to devote himself to official duties with an occasional personal polemic as a relief.   Marvell and Wither, the two
other chief lights of the Puritan party, could hardly be
regarded by any one as men of light and leading, despite
the really charming lyrics which both of them had produced.   All the other great literary names of the time
were, without exception, on the side of the exile.   Hobbes
was a royalist, though a somewhat singular one, Cowley

was a royalist, Herrick was a royalist, so was Denham, so was, as far as he was anything, the unstable Waller. Moreover, the most practically active author of the day, the one man of letters who combined the power of organizing literary effort with the power of himself producing literary work of merit, was one of the staunchest of the king's friends. Sir William Davenant, without any political concession, had somehow obtained leave from the republican government to reintroduce theatrical entertainments of a kind, and moderate royalists, like Evelyn, with an interest in literature and the arts and sciences, were returning to their homes and looking out for the good time coming. That Dryden, under these circumstances, having at the time a much more vivid interest in literature than in politics, and belonging as he did rather to the Presbyterian faction, who were everywhere returning to the royalist political faith, than to the Independent republicans, should become royalist in principle was nothing surprising. Those who reproach him with the change (if change it was) forget that he shared it with the immense majority of the nation. For the last half-century the literary current has been so entirely on the Puritan side that we are probably in danger of doing at least as much injustice to the royalists as was at one time done to their opponents. One thing in particular I have never seen fairly put as accounting for the complete royalization of nearly the whole people, and it is a thing which has a special bearing on Dryden. It has been said that his temperament was specially and exceptionally English. Now one of the most respectable, if not the most purely rational features of the English character, is its objection to wanton bloodshed for political causes, without form of law. It was this beyond all question that alienated

the English from James the Second, it was this that in
the heyday of Hanoverian power made them turn a cold
shoulder on the Duke of Cumberland, it was this which
enlisted them almost as one man against the French
revolutionists, it was this which brought about in our own
days a political movement to which there is no need to
refer more particularly. Now it must be remembered
that either as the losing party, or for other reasons, the
royalists were in the great civil war almost free from the
charge of reckless bloodshedding. Their troops were disorderly and given to plunder, but not to cruelty. No
legend even charges against Astley or Goring, against
Rupert or Lunsford, anything like the Drogheda massacre
—the effect of which on the general mind Defoe, an unexceptionable witness, has preserved by a chance phrase in
Robinson Crusoe—or the hideous bloodbath of the Irish-
women after Naseby, or the brutal butchery of Dr. Hud-
son at Woodcroft in Dryden's own county, where the
soldiers chopped off the priest's fingers as he clung to the
gurgoyles of the tower, and thrust him back with pikes into
the moat which, mutilated as he was, he had managed to
swim. A certain humanity and absence of bloodthirstiness
are among Dryden's most creditable characteristics,[1] and
these excesses of fanaticism are not at all unlikely to have
had their share in determining him to adopt the winning

---

[1] The too famous Political Prologues may, perhaps, be quoted
against me here. I have only to remark : first, that, bad as they
are, they form an infinitesimal portion of Dryden's work, and are
in glaring contrast with the sentiments pervading that work as a
whole ; secondly, that they were written at a time of political
excitement unparalleled in history, save once at Athens and once
or twice at Paris. But I cannot help adding that their de-
nouncers usually seem to me to be at least partially animated by
the notion that Dryden wished the wrong people to be hanged.

side when at last it won. But it is perhaps more to the
purpose that his literary leanings must of themselves have
inevitably inclined him in the same direction. There was
absolutely no opening for literature on the republican side,
a fact of which no better proof can be afforded than the
small salary at which the first man of letters then living
was hired by a government which, whatever faults it had,
certainly did not sin by rewarding its other servants too
meagrely. That Dryden at this time had any deep-set
theological or political prejudices is very improbable. He
certainly had not, like Butler, noted for years the faults
and weaknesses of the dominant party, so as to enshrine
them in immortal ridicule when the time should come.
But he was evidently an ardent devotee of literature ; he
was not averse to the pleasures of the town, which if not
so actively interfered with by the Commonwealth as is
sometimes thought, were certainly not encouraged by it ;
and his friends and associates must have been royalists
almost to a man. So he threw himself at once on that side
when the chance came, and had probably thrown himself
there in spirit some time before. The state of the literature in which he thus took service must be described
before we go any further.

The most convenient division of literature is into poetry,
drama, and prose. With regard to poetry, the reigning
style at the advent of Dryden was, as everybody knows,
the peculiar style unfortunately baptized as " metaphysical." The more catholic criticism of the last 100 years
has disembarrassed this poetry of much of the odium which
once hung round it, without, however, doing full justice
to its merits. In Donne, especially, the king of the
school, the conceits and laboured fancies which distinguish
it frequently reach a hardly surpassed height of poetical

beauty.　When Donne speculates as to the finding on the body of his dead lover

> A bracelet of bright hair about the bone

when he tells us how—

> I long to talk with some old lover's ghost,
> Who died before the god of love was born;

the effect is that of summer lightning on a dark night suddenly exposing unsuspected realms of fantastic and poetical suggestion.　But at its worst the school was certainly bad enough, and its badnesses had already been exhibited by Dryden with considerable felicity in his poem on Lord Hastings and the small-pox.　I really do not know that in all Johnson's carefully picked specimens in his Life of Cowley, a happier absurdity is to be found than

> Each little pimple had a tear in it,
> To wail the fault its rising did commit.

Of such a school as this, though it lent itself more directly than is generally thought to the unequalled oddities of Butler, little good in the way of serious poetry could come.　On the other hand, the great romantic school was practically over, and Milton, its last survivor, was, as has been said, in a state of poetical eclipse.　There was therefore growing up a kind of school of good sense in poetry, of which Waller, Denham, Cowley, and Davenant were the chiefs.　Waller derives most of his fame from his lyrics, inferior as these are to those of Herrick and Carew. Cowley was a metaphysician with a strong hankering after something different.　Denham, having achieved one admirable piece of versification, had devoted himself chiefly to

doggrel; but Davenant, though perhaps not so good a
poet as any of the three, was a more living influence. His
early works, especially his dirge on Shakespeare and his
exquisite lines to the Queen, are of the best stamp of the
older school. His *Gondibert*, little as it is now read, and
unsuccessful as the quatrain in which it is written must
always be for a very long work, is better than any long
narrative poem, for many a year before and after. Both
his poetical and his dramatic activity (of which more
anon) were incessant, and were almost always exerted in the
direction of innovation. But the real importance of these
four writers was the help they gave to the development of
the heroic couplet, the predestined common form of
poetry of the more important kind for a century and a
half to come. The heroic couplet was, of course, no
novelty in English; but it had hitherto been only fitfully
patronized for poems of length, and had not been adapted
for general use. The whole structure of the decasyllabic
line before the middle of the seventeenth century, was ill
calculated for the perfecting of the couplet. Accustomed
either to the stately plainness of blank verse, or to the
elaborate intricacies of the stanza, writers had got into the
habit of communicating to their verse a slow and somewhat
languid movement. The satiric poems in which the couplet
had been most used were, either by accident or design,
couched in the roughest possible verse, so rough that in
the hands of Marston and Donne it almost ceased to be
capable of scansion. In general, the couplet had two drawbacks. Either it was turned by means of *enjambements* into
something very like rhythmic prose, with rhymes straying
about at apparently indefinite intervals, or it was broken
up into a *staccato* motion by the neglect to support and carry
on the rhythm at the termination of the distichs. All the

four poets mentioned, especially the three first, did much
to fit the couplet for miscellaneous work. All of them
together, it is hardly needful to say, did not do so much
as the young Cambridge man who, while doing bookseller's work for Herringman the publisher, hanging about
the coffee-houses, and planning plays with Davenant and
Sir Robert Howard, was waiting for opportunity and impulse to help him to make his way.

The drama was in an even more critical state than
poetry pure and simple, and here Davenant was the
important person. All the giant race except Shirley were
dead, and Shirley had substituted a kind of *tragédie
bourgeoise* for the work of his masters. Other practitioners
chiefly favoured the example of one of the least imitable
of those masters, and out-forded Ford in horrors of all
kinds, while the comedians clung still more tightly to the
humour-comedy of Jonson. Davenant himself had made
abundant experiments—experiments, let it be added,
sometimes of no small merit—in both these styles. But
the occupations of tragedy and comedy were gone, and
the question was how to find a new one for them. Davenant succeeded in procuring permission from the Protector,
who like most Englishmen of the time was fond of music,
to give what would now be called entertainments; and
the entertainments soon developed into something like
regular stage plays. But Shakespeare's godson, with his
keen manager's appreciation of the taste of the public,
and his travelled experience, did not content himself with
deviating cautiously into the old paths. He it was who,
in the *Siege of Rhodes*, introduced at once into England
the opera, and a less long-lived but, in a literary point
of view, more important variety, the heroic play, the latter
of which always retained some tinge of the former. There

are not many subjects on 'which, to put it plainly, more rubbish has been talked than the origin of the heroic play. Very few Englishmen have ever cared to examine accurately the connexion between this singular growth and the classical tragedy already flourishing in France ; still fewer have ever cared to investigate the origins of that classical tragedy itself. The blundering attribution of Dryden and his rivals to Corneille and Racine, the more blundering attribution of Corneille and Racine to the Scudéry romance (as if somebody should father Shelley on Monk Lewis) has been generally accepted without much hesitation, though Dryden himself has pointed out that there is but little connexion between the French and the English drama ; and though the history of the French drama itself is perfectly intel-ligible, and by no means difficult to trace. The French classical drama is the direct descendant of the drama of Seneca, first imitated by Jodelle and Garnier in the days of the *Pléiade ;* nor did it ever quit that model, though in the first thirty years of the seventeenth century something was borrowed from Spanish sources. The English heroic drama, on the other hand, which Davenant invented, which Sir Robert Howard and Lord Orrery made fashionable, and for which Dryden achieved a popularity of nearly twenty years, was one of the most cosmopolitan—I had almost said the most mongrel—of literary productions. It adopted the English freedom of action, multiplicity of character, and licence of stirring scenes acted *coram populo.* It borrowed lyrical admixture from Italy, exaggerated and bombastic language came to it from Spain, and to France it owed little more than its rhymed dialogue, and perhaps something of its sighs and flames. The disadvantages of rhyme in dramatic writing seem to modern Englishmen

so great, that they sometimes find it difficult to understand
how any rational being could exchange the blank verse
of Shakespeare for the rhymes of Dryden, much more
for the rhymes of his contemporaries and predecessors.
But this omits the important consideration that it was not
the blank verse of Shakespeare or of Fletcher that was
thus exchanged. In the three-quarters of a century, or
thereabouts, which elapsed between the beginning of the
great dramatic era and the Restoration, the chief vehicle
of the drama had degenerated full as much as the drama
itself; and the blank verse of the plays subsequent to
Ford is of anything but Shakespearian quality—is indeed
in many cases such as is hardly to be recognized for verse
at all. Between this awkward and inharmonious stuff
and the comparatively polished and elegant couplets of
the innovators there could be little comparison, especially
when Dryden had taken up the couplet himself.

Lastly, in prose the time was pretty obviously calling
for a reform. There were great masters of English prose
living when Dryden joined the literary world of London,
but there was no generally accepted style for the journeywork of literature. Milton and Taylor could arrange the
most elaborate symphonies; Hobbes could write with a
crabbed clearness as lucid almost as the flowing sweetness
of Berkeley; but these were exceptions. The endless sentences out of which Clarendon is wont just to save himself,
when his readers are wondering whether breath and brain
will last out their involution; the hopeless coils of parenthesis and afterthought in which Cromwell's speech lay
involved, till Mr. Carlyle was sent on a special mission
to disentangle them, show the dangers and difficulties
of the ordinary prose style of the day. It was terribly
cumbered about quotations, which it introduced with

merciless frequency. It had no notion of a unit of style
in the sentence. It indulged, without the slightest hesitation, in every *détour* and involution of second thoughts
and by-the-way qualifications. So far as any models were
observed, those models were chiefly taken from the in-
flected languages of Greece and Rome, where the structural
alterations of the words according to their grammatical
connexion are for the most part sufficient to make the
meaning tolerably clear. Nothing so much as the lack of
inflexions saved our prose at this time from sharing the
fate of German, and involving itself almost beyond the
reach of extrication. The common people, when not bent
upon fine language, could speak and write clearly and
straighforwardly, as Bunyan's works show to this day to
all who care to read. But scholars and divines deserved
much less well of their mother tongue. It may indeed be
said that prose was infinitely worse off than poetry. In
the latter there had been an excellent style, if not one
perfectly suited for all ends, and it had degenerated. In the
former, nothing like a general prose style had ever yet
been elaborated at all; what had been done had been done
chiefly in the big-bow-wow manner, as Dryden's editor
might have called it. For light miscellaneous work,
neither fantastic nor solemn, the demand was only just
being created. Cowley indeed wrote well, and, comparatively speaking, elegantly, but his prose work was small in
extent and little read in comparison to his verse. Tillotson was Dryden's own contemporary, and hardly preceded
him in the task of reform.

From this short notice it will be obvious that the
general view, according to which a considerable change
took place and was called for at the Restoration, is correct,
notwithstanding the attempts recently made to prove the

contrary by a learned writer.   Professor Masson's lists of
men of letters and of the dates of their publication of
their works prove, if he will pardon my saying so, nothing.
The actual spirit of the time is to be judged not from the
production of works of writers who, as they one by one
dropped off, left no successors, but from those who struck
root downwards and blossomed upwards in the general
literary soil.   Milton is not a writer of the Restoration,
though his greatest works appeared after it, and though he
survived it nearly fifteen years.   Nor was Taylor, nor
Clarendon, nor Cowley : hardly even Davenant, or Waller,
or Butler, or Denham.   The writers of the Restoration are
those whose works had the seeds of life in them ; who divined
or formed the popular tastes of the period, who satisfied
that taste, and who trained up successors to prosecute and
modify their own work.   The interval between the prose
and the poetry of Dryden and the prose and the poetry of
Milton is that of an entire generation, notwithstanding
the manner in which, chronologically speaking, they overlap.
The objects which the reformer, consciously or unconsciously, set before him have been sufficiently indicated.
It must be the task of the following chapters to show how
and to what extent he effected a reform ; what the nature of
that reform was ; what was the value of the work which
in effecting it he contributed to the literature of his
country.

CHAPTER II.

EARLY LITERARY WORK.

THE foregoing chapter will have already shown the chief difficulty of writing a life of Dryden—the almost entire absence of materials. At the Restoration the poet was nearly thirty years old, and of positive information as to his life during these thirty years we have half a dozen dates, the isolated fact of his mishap at Trinity, a single letter and three poems, not amounting in all to three hundred lines. Nor can it be said that even subsequently, during his forty years of fame and literary activity, positive information as to his life is plentiful. His works are still the best life of him, and in so far as a biography of Dryden is filled with any matter not purely literary, it must for the most part be filled with controversy as to his political and religious opinions and conduct rather than with accounts of his actual life and conversation. Omitting for the present literary work, the next fact that we have to record after the Restoration is one of some importance, though as before the positive information obtainable in connexion with it is but scanty. On the 1st of December, 1663, Dryden was married at St. Swithin's Church to Lady Elizabeth Howard, eldest daughter of the Earl of Berkshire.

This marriage, like most of the scanty events of Dryden's

life, has been made the occasion of much and unnecessary controversy. The libellers of the Popish Plot disturbances twenty years later declared that the character of the bride was doubtful, and that her brothers had acted towards Dryden in somewhat the same way as the Hamiltons did towards Grammont. A letter of hers to the Earl of Chesterfield, which was published about half a century ago, has been used to support the first charge, besides abundant arguments as to the unlikelihood of an earl's daughter marrying a poor poet for love. It is one of the misfortunes of prominent men that when fact is silent about their lives fiction is always busy. If we brush away the cobwebs of speculation, there is nothing in the least suspicious about this matter. Lord Berkshire had a large family and a small property. Dryden himself was, as we have seen, well born and well connected. That some of his sisters had married tradesmen seems to Scott likely to have been shocking to the Howards; but he must surely have forgotten the famous story of the Earl of Bedford's objection to be raised a step in the peerage because it would make it awkward for the younger scions of the house of Russell to go into trade. The notion of an absolute severance between Court and City at that time, is one of the many unhistorical fictions which have somehow or other obtained currency. Dryden was already an intimate friend of Sir Robert Howard, if not also of the other brother, Edward, and perhaps it is not unnoteworthy that Lady Elizabeth was five-and-twenty, an age in those days somewhat mature, and one at which a young lady would be thought wise by her family in accepting any creditable offer. As to the Chesterfield letter, the evidence it contains can only satisfy minds previously made up. It testifies certainly to something like a flirtation, and suggests an interview, but there

is nothing in it at all compromising.   The libels already
mentioned are perfectly vague and wholly untrustworthy.

It seems, though on no very definite evidence, that the
marriage was not altogether a happy one.   Dryden appears
to have acquired some small property in Wiltshire ;
perhaps also a royal grant which was made to Lady
Elizabeth in recognition of her father's services ; and Lord
Berkshire's Wiltshire house of Charlton became a country
retreat for the poet.   But his wife was, it is said, ill-tempered
and not overburdened with brains, and he himself was probably no more a model of conjugal propriety than most of
his associates.   I say probably, for here, too, it is astonishing how the evidence breaks down when it is examined, or
rather how it vanishes altogether into air.   Mr. J. R.
Green has roundly informed the world that " Dryden's life
was that of a libertine, and his marriage with a woman
who was yet more dissolute than himself only gave a new
spur to his debaucheries."   We have seen what foundation there is for this gross charge against Lady Elizabeth ;
now let us see what ground there is for the charge against
Dryden.   There are the libels of Shadwell and the rest of
the crew, to which not even Mr. Christie, a very severe
judge of Dryden's moral character, assigns the slightest
weight ; there is the immorality ascribed to Bayes in the
Rehearsal, a very pretty piece of evidence indeed, seeing
that Bayes is a confused medley of half a dozen persons ;
there is a general association by tradition of Dryden's
name with that of Mrs. Reeve, a beautiful actress of the
day ; and finally there is a tremendous piece of scandal
which is the battle-horse of the devil's advocates.   A
curious letter appeared in the *Gentleman's Magazine* for
1745, the author of which is unknown, though conjec-
tures, as to which there are difficulties, identify him with

Dryden's youthful friend Southern. " I remember," says
this person, "plain John Dryden, before he paid his court
with success to the great, in one uniform clothing of Nor-
wich drugget. I have ate tarts with him and Madam
Reeve at the Mulberry Garden, when our author advanced
to a sword and a Chedreux wig." Perhaps there is no
more curious instance of the infinitesimal foundation on
which scandal builds than this matter of Dryden's immorality. Putting aside mere vague libellous declamation, the
one piece of positive information on the subject that we
have is anonymous, was made at least seventy years after
date, and avers that John Dryden, a dramatic author, once
ate tarts with an actress and a third person. This translated into the language of Mr. Green becomes the disso-
luteness of a libertine, spurred up to new debaucheries.

It is immediately after the marriage that we have almost
our first introduction to Dryden as a live man seen by live
human beings. And the circumstances of this introduction are characteristic enough. On the 3rd of February,
1664, Pepys tells us that he stopped, as he was going to
fetch his wife, at the great coffee-house in Covent Garden,
and there he found "Dryden, the poet I knew at Cambridge," and all the wits of the town. The company
pleased Pepys, and he made a note to the effect, that " it
will be good coming thither." But the most interesting
thing is this glimpse, first, of the associates of Dryden at
the university; secondly, of his installation at Will's,
the famous house of call, where he was later to reign as
undisputed monarch ; and thirdly, of the fact that he was
already recognized as "Dryden the poet." The remainder
of the present chapter will best be occupied by pointing
out what he had done, and in brief space afterwards, did
do, to earn that title, reserving the important subject of

his dramatic activity, which also began about this time,
for separate treatment.

The lines on the death of Lord Hastings, and the lines
to Hoddesdon, have, it has been said, a certain promise
about them to experienced eyes, but it is of that kind of
promise which, as the same experience teaches, is at least
as often followed by little performance as by much. The
lines on Cromwell deserve less faint praise. The following
stanzas exhibit at once the masculine strength and originality which were to be the poet's great sources of power,
and the habit of conceited and pedantic allusion which he
had caught from the fashions of the time :—

> Swift and resistless through the land he passed,
>   Like that bold Greek who did the East subdue,
> And made to battle such heroic haste
>   As if on wings of victory he flew.
>
> He fought secure of fortune as of fame,
>   Till by new maps the island might be shown
> Of conquests, which he strewed where'er he came,
>   Thick as the galaxy with stars is sown.
>
> His palms, though under weights they did not stand,
>   Still thrived ; no winter did his laurels fade.
> Heaven in his portrait showed a workman's hand,
>   And drew it perfect, yet without a shade.
>
> Peace was the prize of all his toil and care,
>   Which war had banished, and did now restore :
> Bologna's walls so mounted in the air
>   To seat themselves more surely than before.

An impartial contemporary critic, if he could have anticipated the methods of a later school of criticism, might
have had some difficulty in deciding whether the masterly

plainness, directness, and vigour of the best lines here ought
or ought not to excuse the conceit about the palms and
the weights, and the fearfully far-fetched piece of fancy history about Bologna. Such a critic, if he had had the better
part of discretion, would have decided in the affirmative.
There were not three poets then living who could have
written the best lines of the Heroic Stanzas, and what is
more, those lines were not in the particular manner of either
of the poets who, as far as general poetical merit goes,
might have written them. But the Restoration, which
for reasons given already I must hold to have been
genuinely welcome to Dryden, and not a mere occasion of
profitable coat-turning, brought forth some much less
ambiguous utterances. *Astræa Redux* (1660), a panegyric
on the coronation (1661), a poem to Lord Clarendon
(1662), a few still shorter pieces of the complimentary
kind to Dr. Charleton (1663), to the Duchess of York
(1665), and to Lady Castlemaine (166–?), lead up to *Annus
Mirabilis* at the beginning of 1667, the crowning effort of
Dryden's first poetical period, and his last before the long
absorption in purely dramatic occupations which lasted
till the Popish Plot and its controversies evoked from him
the expression of hitherto unsuspected powers.

These various pieces do not amount in all to more than
two thousand lines, of which nearly two-thirds belong to
Annus Mirabilis. But they were fully sufficient to show
that a new poetical power had arisen in the land, and their
qualities, good and bad, might have justified the anticipa-
tion that the writer would do better and better work as
he grew older. All the pieces enumerated, with the exception of *Annus Mirabilis*, are in the heroic couplet, and
their versification is of such a kind that the relapse into
the quatrain in the longer poem is not a little surprising.

But nothing is more characteristic of Dryden than the extremely tentative character of his work, and he had doubtless not yet satisfied himself that the couplet was suitable for narrative poems of any length, notwithstanding the mastery over it which he must have known himself to have attained in his short pieces. The very first lines of *Astræa Redux* show this mastery clearly enough.

> Now with a general peace the world was blest,
> While ours, a world divided from the rest,
> A dreadful quiet felt, and worser far
> Than arms, a sullen interval of war.

Here is already the energy divine for which the author was to be famed, and, in the last line at least, an instance of the varied cadence and subtly-disposed music which were, in his hands, to free the couplet from all charges of monotony and tameness. But almost immediately there is a falling off. The poet goes off into an unnecessary simile preceded by the hackneyed and clumsy " thus," a simile quite out of place at the opening of a poem, and disfigured by the too famous, " an horrid stillness first invades the ear," which if it has been extravagantly blamed —and it seems to me that it has—certainly will go near to be thought a conceit. But we have not long to wait for another chord that announces Dryden :—

> For his long absence Church and State did groan,
> Madness the pulpit, faction seized the throne.
> Experienced age in deep despair was lost
> To see the rebel thrive, the loyal crost.
> Youth, that with joys had unacquainted been,
> Envied grey hairs that once good days had seen.
> We thought our sires, not with their own content,
> Had, ere we came to age, our portion spent.

Whether the matter of this is suitable for poetry or not is

one of those questions on which doctors will doubtless
disagree to the end of the chapter. But even when we
look back through the long rows of practitioners of the
couplet who have succeeded Dryden, we shall, I think,
hardly find one who is capable of such masterly treatment
of the form, of giving to the phrase a turn at once so
clear and so individual, of weighting the verse with such
dignity, and at the same time winging it with such lightly
flying speed. The poem is injured by numerous passages
introduced by the usual "as" and "thus" and "like,"
which were intended for ornaments, and which in fact
simply disfigure. It is here and there charged, after the
manner of the day, with inappropriate and clumsy learning, and with doubtful Latinisms of expression. But it is
redeemed by such lines as—

> When to be God's anointed was his crime ;

as the characteristic gibe at the Covenant insinuated by the
description of the Guisean League—

> As holy and as Catholic as ours ;

as the hit at the

> Polluted nest
> Whence legion twice before was dispossest ;

as the splendid couplet on the British Amphitrite—

> Proud her returning prince to entertain
> With the submitted fasces of the main.

Such lines as these must have had for the readers of 1660
the attraction of a novelty which only very careful stu-
dents of the literature of the time can understand now.
The merits of *Astræa Redux* must of course not be judged
by the reader's acquiescence in its sentiments. But let

any one read the following passage without thinking of the
treaty of Dover and the closed exchequer, of Madam Car-
well's twelve thousand a year, and Lord Russell's scaffold,
and he assuredly will not fail to recognise their beauty :—

> Methinks I see those crowds on Dover's strand,
> Who in their haste to welcome you to land
> Choked up the beach with their still-growing store,
> And made a wilder torrent on the shore :
> While, spurred with eager thoughts of past delight,
> Those who had seen you court a second sight,
> Preventing still your steps, and making haste
> To meet you often wheresoe'er you past.
> How shall I speak of that triumphant day
> When you renewed the expiring pomp of May ?
> A month that owns an interest in your name ;
> You and the flowers are its peculiar claim.
> That star, that at your birth shone out so bright
> It stained the duller sun's meridian light,
> Did once again its potent fires renew,
> Guiding our eyes to find and worship you.

The extraordinary art with which the recurrences of the
you and *your*—in the circumstances naturally recited with
a little stress of the voice—are varied in position so as to
give a corresponding variety to the cadence of the verse,
is perhaps the chief thing to be noted here. But a comparison with even the best couplet verse of the time will
show many other excellences in it. I am aware that this
style of minute criticism has gone out of fashion, and that
the variations of the position of a pronoun have terribly
little to do with " criticism of life ;" but as I am dealing
with a great English author whose main distinction is to
have reformed the whole formal part of English prose and
English poetry, I must, once for all, take leave to follow
the only road open to me to show what he actually did.

The other smaller couplet-poems which have been

mentioned are less important than *Astræa Redux*, not merely in point of size, but because they are later in date The piece on the coronation, however, contains lines and passages equal to any in the longer poem, and it shows very happily the modified form of conceit which Dryden, throughout his life, was fond of employing, and which, employed with his judgment and taste, fairly escapes the charges usually brought against "Clevelandisms," while it helps to give to the heroic the colour and picturesqueness which after the days of Pope it too often lacked. Such is the fancy about the postponement of the ceremony—

> Had greater haste these sacred rites prepared
> Some guilty months had in our triumph shared.
> But this untainted year is all your own,
> Your glories may without our crimes be shown.

And such an exceedingly fine passage in the poem to Clarendon which is one of the most finished pieces of Dryden's early versification—

> Our setting sun from his declining seat
> Shot beams of kindness on you, not of heat :
> And, when his love was bounded in a few
> That were unhappy that they might be true,
> Made you the favourite of his last sad times,
> That is, a sufferer in his subjects' crimes :
> Thus those first favours you received were sent,
> Like Heaven's rewards, in earthly punishment.
> Yet Fortune, conscious of your destiny,
> Even then took care to lay you softly by,
> And wrapt your fate among her precious things,
> Kept fresh to be unfolded with your King's.
> Shown all at once, you dazzled so our eyes
> As new-born Pallas did the god's surprise ;
> When springing forth from Jove's new-closing wound,
> She struck the warlike spear into the ground ;
> Which sprouting leaves did suddenly enclose
> And peaceful olives shaded as they rose.

For once the mania for simile and classical allusion has not led the author astray here, but has furnished him with a very happy and legitimate ornament. The only fault in the piece is the use of " did," which Dryden never wholly discarded, and which is perhaps occasionally allowable enough.

The remaining poems require no very special remark, though all contain evidence of the same novel and unmatched mastery over the couplet and its cadence. The author, however, was giving himself more and more to the dramatic studies which will form the subject of the next chapter, and to the prose criticisms which almost from the first he associated with those studies. But the events of the year 1666 tempted him once more to indulge in non-dramatic work, and the poem of *Annus Mirabilis* was the result. It seems to have been written, in part at least, at Lord Berkshire's seat of Charlton, close to Malmesbury, and was prefaced by a letter to Sir Robert Howard. Dryden appears to have lived at Charlton during the greater part of 1665 and 1666, the plague and fire years. He had been driven from London, not merely by dread of the pestilence, but by the fact that his ordinary occupation was gone owing to the closing of the play-houses, and he evidently occupied himself at Charlton with a good deal of literary work, including his essay on dramatic poetry, his play of the *Maiden Queen*, and *Annus Mirabilis* itself. This last was published very early in 1667, and seems to have been successful. Pepys bought it on the 2nd of February, and was fortunately able to like it better than he did *Hudibras*. " A very good poem," the Clerk of the Acts of the Navy writes it down. It may be mentioned in passing that during this same stay at Charlton Dryden's eldest son Charles was born.

Annus Mirabilis consists of 304 quatrains on the *Gondi-bert* model, reasons for the adoption of which Dryden gives (not so forcibly perhaps as is usual with him) in the before-mentioned letter to his brother-in-law. He speaks of rhyme generally with less respect than he was soon to show, and declares that he has adopted the quatrain because he judges it " more noble and full of dignity " than any other form he knows. The truth seems to be that he was still to a great extent under the influence of Davenant, and that *Gondibert* as yet retained sufficient pres-tige to make its stanza act as a not unfavourable advertise-ment of poems written in it. With regard to the nobility and dignity of this stanza, it may safely be said that *Annus Mirabilis* itself, the best poem ever written therein, killed it by exposing its faults. It is indeed, at least when the rhymes of the stanzas are unconnected, a very bad metre for the purpose. For it is chargeable with more than the dis-jointedness of the couplet, without the possibility of relief, while on the other hand the quatrains have not, like the Spenserian stave or the *ottava rima*, sufficient bulk to form units in themselves, and to include within them varieties of harmony. Despite these drawbacks, however, Dryden produced a very fine poem in *Annus Mirabilis*, though I am not certain that even its best passages equal those cited from the couplet pieces. At any rate in this poem the characteristics of the master in what may be called his poetical adolescence are displayed to the fullest extent. The weight and variety of his line, his abundance of illus-tration and fancy, his happy turns of separate phrase, and his singular faculty of bending to poetical uses the most refractory names and things, all make themselves fully felt here. On the other hand there is still an undue tendency to conceit and exuberance of simile. The famous lines—

> These fight like husbands, but like lovers those ;
> These fain would keep, and those more fain enjoy ;

are followed in the next stanza by a most indubitably
" metaphysical " statement that

> Some preciously by shattered porcelain fall
> And some by aromatic splinters die.

This cannot be considered the happiest possible means of
informing us that the Dutch fleet was laden with spices
and *magots*. Such puerile fancies are certainly unworthy
of a poet who could tell how

> The mighty ghosts of our great Harrys rose
> And armèd Edwards looked with anxious eyes ;

and who, in the beautiful simile of the eagle, has equalled
the Elizabethans at their own weapons. I cannot think,
however, admirable as the poem is in its best passages
(the description of the fire for instance), that it is
technically the equal of *Astræa Redux*. The monotonous
recurrence of the same identical cadence in each stanza—
a recurrence which even Dryden's art was unable to prevent, and which can only be prevented by some such
interlacements of rhymes and *enjambements* of sense as
those which Mr. Swinburne has successfully adopted in
Laus Veneris—injures the best passages. The best of all
is undoubtedly the following :—

> In this deep quiet, from what source unknown,
>   Those seeds of fire their fatal birth disclose ;
> And first few scattering sparks about were blown,
>   Big with the flames that to our ruin rose.
>
> Then in some close-pent room it crept along
>   And, smouldering as it went, in silence fed ;
> Till the infant monster, with devouring strong,
>   Walked boldly upright with exalted head.

Now, like some rich and mighty murderer,
 Too great for prison which he breaks with gold,
Who fresher for new mischiefs does appear
 And dares the world to tax him with the old,

So 'scapes the insulting fire his narrow jail
 And makes small outlets into open air;
There the fierce winds his tender force assail
 And beat him downward to his first repair.

The winds, like crafty courtesans, withheld
 His flames from burning but to blow them more:
And, every fresh attempt, he is repelled
 With faint denials, weaker than before.

And now, no longer letted of his prey
 He leaps up at it with enraged desire,
O'erlooks the neighbours with a wide survey
 And nods at every house his threatening fire.

The ghosts of traitors from the Bridge descend,
 With bold fanatic spectres to rejoice;
About the fire into a dance they bend
 And sing their sabbath notes with feeble voice.

The last stanza indeed contains a fine image finely expressed, but I cannot but be glad that Dryden tried no more experiments with the recalcitrant quatrain.

Annus Mirabilis closes the series of early poems, and for fourteen years from the date of its publication Dryden was known, with insignificant exceptions, as a dramatic writer only. But his efforts in poetry proper, though they had not as yet resulted in any masterpiece, had, as I have endeavoured to point out, amply entitled him to the position of a great and original master of the formal part of poetry, if not of a poet who had distinctly found his way. He had carried out a conception of the couplet which was almost entirely new, having been anticipated only by some isolated and ill-sustained efforts. He had manifested an equal originality in the turn of his phrase, an extraordinary command of poetic imagery, and, above all, a faculty of handling by no means promising subjects in an indisputably poetical manner. Circumstances which I shall now proceed to describe called him away from the practice of pure poetry, leaving to him, however, a reputation amply deserved and acknowledged even by his enemies, of possessing unmatched skill in versification. Nor were the studies upon which he now entered wholly alien to his proper function, though they were in some sort a bye-work. They strengthened his command over the language, increased his skill in verse, and above all tended by degrees to reduce and purify what was corrupt in his phraseology and system of ornamentation. Fourteen years of dramatic practice did more than turn out some admirable scenes and some even more admirable criticism. They acted as a filtering reservoir for his poetical powers, so that the stream which, when it ran into them, was the turbid and rubbish-laden current of *Annus Mirabilis* flowed out as impetuous, as strong, but clear and without base admixture, in the splendid verse of *Absalom and Achitophel.*

CHAPTER III.

PERIOD OF DRAMATIC ACTIVITY.

THERE are not many portions of English literature which
have been treated with greater severity by critics than
the Restoration drama, and of the Restoration dramatists
few have met with less favour, in proportion to their
general literary eminence, than Dryden. Of his comedies
in particular few have been found to say a good word.
His sturdiest champion, Scott, dismisses them as "heavy;"
Hazlitt, a defender of the Restoration comedy in general,
finds little in them but "ribaldry and extravagance;"
and I have lately seen them spoken of with a shudder as
"horrible." The tragedies have fared better, but not
much better; and thus the remarkable spectacle is
presented of a general condemnation, varied only by
the faintest praise, of the work to which an admitted
master of English devoted, almost exclusively, twenty
years of the flower of his manhood. So complete is the
oblivion into which these dramas have fallen, that it has
buried in its folds the always charming and sometimes
exquisite songs which they contain. Except in Congreve's
two editions, and in the bulky edition of Scott, Dryden's
theatre is unattainable, and thus the majority of readers
have but little opportunity of correcting from individual
study the unfavourable impressions derived from the

verdicts of the critics. For myself, I am very far from considering Dryden's dramatic work as on a level with his purely poetical work. But as nearly always happens, and as happened, by a curious coincidence, in the case of his editor, the fact that he did something else much better has obscured the fact that he did this thing in not a few instances very well. Scott's poems as poems are far inferior to his novels as novels; Dryden's plays are far inferior as plays to his satires and his fables as poems. But both the poems of Scott and the plays of Dryden are a great deal better than the average critic admits.

That dramatic work went somewhat against the grain with Dryden, is frequently asserted on his own authority, and is perhaps true. He began it, however, tolerably early, and had finished at least the scheme of a play (on a subject which he afterwards resumed) shortly after the Restoration. As soon as that event happened, a double incentive to play-writing began to work upon him. It was much the most fashionable of literary occupations, and also much the most lucrative. Dryden was certainly not indifferent to fame, and, though he was by no means a covetous man, he seems to have possessed at all times the perfect readiness to spend whatever could be honestly got which frequently distinguishes men of letters. He set to work accordingly, and produced in 1663 the *Wild Gallant*. We do not possess this play in the form in which it was first acted and damned. Afterwards Lady Castlemaine gave it her protection; the author added certain attractions according to the taste of the time, and it was both acted and published. It certainly cannot be said to be a great success even as it is. Dryden had, like most of his fellows, attempted the Comedy of Humours,

as it was called at the time, and as it continued to be,
and to be called, till the more polished comedy of
manners, or artificial comedy, succeeded it, owing to the
success of Wycherley, and still more of Congreve. The
number of comedies of this kind written after 1620 is
very large, while the fantastic and poetical comedy of
which Shakespeare and Fletcher had almost alone the
secret had almost entirely died out. The merit of the
Comedy of Humours is the observation of actual life
which it requires in order to be done well, and the
consequent fidelity with which it holds up the muses'
looking-glass (to use the title of one of Randolph's plays)
to nature. Its defects are its proneness to descend into
farce, and the temptation which it gives to the writer to
aim rather at mere fragmentary and sketchy delineations
than at finished composition. At the Restoration this school
of drama was vigorously enough represented by Davenant
himself, by Sir Aston Cokain, and by Wilson, a writer of
great merit who rather unaccountably abandoned the stage
very soon, while in a year or two Shadwell, the actor Lacy
and several others were to take it up and carry it on. It
had frequently been combined with the embroiled and
complicated plots of the Spanish comedy of intrigue, the
adapters usually allowing these plots to conduct themselves
much more irregularly than was the case in the originals,
while the deficiencies were made up, or supposed to be
made up, by a liberal allowance of " humours." The
danger of this sort of work was perhaps never better
illustrated than by Shadwell, when he boasted in one of
his prefaces that " four of the humours were entirely
new," and appeared to consider this a sufficient claim to
respectful reception. Dryden in his first play fell to the
fullest extent into the blunder of this combined Spanish-

English style, though on no subsequent occasion did he
repeat the mistake.   By degrees the example and influence
of Molière sent complicated plots and "humours" alike
out of fashion, though the national taste and temperament
were too strongly in favour of the latter to allow them to
be totally banished.   In our very best plays of the so-called
artificial style, such as *Love for Love*, and the master-
pieces of Sheridan, character sketches to which Ben Jonson
himself would certainly not refuse the title of humours
appear, and contribute a large portion of the interest.
Dryden, however, was not likely to anticipate this better
time, or even to distinguish himself in the older form of
the humour-comedy.   He had little aptitude for the odd
and quaint, nor had he any faculty of devising or picking
up strokes of extravagance, such as those which his enemy
Shadwell could command, though he could make no very
good use of them.   The humours of Trice and Bibber
and Lord Nonsuch in the *Wild Gallant* are forced and
too often feeble, though there are flashes here and there,
especially in the part of Sir Timorous, a weakling of the
tribe of Aguecheek; but in this first attempt, the one
situation and the one pair of characters which Dryden
was to treat with tolerable success are already faintly
sketched.   In Constance and Loveby, the pair of light-
hearted lovers who carry on a flirtation without too much
modesty certainly, and with a remarkable absence of re-
finement, but at the same time with some genuine affection
for one another and in a hearty, natural manner, make their
first appearance.   It is to be noted in Dryden's favour that
these lovers of his are for the most part free from the
charge of brutal heartlessness and cruelty, which has
been justly brought against those of Etherege, of
Wycherley, and, at least in the case of the *Old Bachelor*,

of Congreve. The men are rakes, and rather vulgar
rakes, but they are nothing worse. The women have too
many of the characteristics of Charles the Second's maids
of honour ; but they have, at the same time, a certain
healthiness and sweetness of the older days, which bring
them, if not close to Rosalind and Beatrice, at any rate
pretty near to Fletcher's heroines, such as Dorothea and
Mary. Still the *Wild Gallant* can by no possibility be
called a good play. It was followed, at no long interval,
by the *Rival Ladies*, a tragicomedy, which is chiefly
remarkable for containing some heroic scenes in rhyme,
for imitating closely the tangled and improbable plot of
its Spanish original, for being tolerably decent, and I
fear it must be added, for being intolerably dull. The
third venture was in every way more important. The
Indian Emperor (1665) was Dryden's first original play, his
first heroic play, and indirectly formed part of a curious
literary dispute, one of many in which he was engaged,
but which in this case proved fertile in critical studies of
his best brand. Sir Robert Howard, Dryden's brother-in-
law, had with the assistance of Dryden himself, produced
a play called the *Indian Queen*, and to this the *Indian
Emperor* was nominally a sequel. But as Dryden remarks,
with a quaintness which may or may not be satirical, the
conclusion of the *Indian Queen* " left but little matter to
build upon, there remaining but two of the considerable
characters alive." The good Sir Robert had indeed
heaped the stage with dead in his last act in a manner
which must have confirmed any French critic who saw or
read the play in his belief of the bloodthirstiness of the
English drama. The field was thus completely clear, and
Dryden, retaining only Montezuma as his hero, used his
own fancy and invention without restraint in constructing

the plot and arranging the characters. The play was
extremely popular, and it divides with *Tyrannic Love* and
the *Conquest of Granada* the merit of being the best of
all English heroic plays. The origin of that singular
growth has been already given, and there is no need to
repeat the story, while the *Conquest of Granada* is so much
more the model play of the style, that anything like an
analysis of a heroic play had better be reserved for this.
The *Indian Emperor* was followed, in 1667, by the
Maiden Queen, a tragicomedy. The tragic or heroic
part is very inferior to its predecessor, but the comic
part has merits which are by no means inconsiderable.
Celadon and Florimel are the first finished specimens of
that pair of practitioners of light o' love flirtation which
was Dryden's sole contribution of any value to the
comic stage. Charles gave the play particular commendation, and called it " his play," as Dryden takes care
to tell us. Still in the same year came *Sir Martin Mar-
all*, Dryden's second pure comedy. But it is in no
sense an original play, and Dryden was not even the
original adapter. The Duke of Newcastle, famous equally
for his own gallantry in the civil war and for the
oddities of his second duchess, Margaret Lucas, translated
l'Etourdi, and gave it to Dryden, who perhaps combined
with it some things taken from other French plays, added
not a little of his own, and had it acted. It was for
those days exceedingly successful, running more than
thirty nights at its first appearance. It is very coarse in
parts, but amusing enough. The English blunderer is a
much more contemptible person than his French original.
He is punished instead of being rewarded, and there is a
great deal of broad farce brought in. Dryden was about
this time frequently engaged in this doubtful sort of col-

laboration, and the very next play which he produced, also a result of it, has done his reputation more harm than any other. This was the disgusting burlesque of the *Tempest*, which, happily, there is much reason for thinking belongs almost wholly to Davenant. Besides degrading in every way the poetical merit of the poem, Sir William, from whom better things might have been expected, got into his head what Dryden amiably calls the "excellent contrivance" of giving Miranda a sister, and inventing a boy (Hippolito) who has never seen a woman. The excellent contrivance gives rise to a good deal of extremely characteristic wit. But here, too, there is little reason for giving Dryden credit or discredit for anything more than a certain amount of arrangement and revision. His next appearance, in 1668, with the *Mock Astrologer* was a more independent one. He was indeed, as was very usual with him, indebted to others for the main points of his play, which comes partly from Thomas Corneille's *Feint Astrologue*, partly from the *Dépit Amoureux*. But the play, with the usual reservations, may be better spoken of than any of Dryden's comedies, except *Marriage à la Mode* and *Amphitryon*. Wildblood and Jacintha, who play the parts of Celadon and Florimel in the *Maiden Queen*, are a very lively pair. Much of the dialogue is smart, and the incidents are stirring, while the play contains no less than four of the admirable songs which Dryden now began to lavish on his audiences. In the same year, or perhaps in 1669, appeared the play of *Tyrannic Love*, or the *Royal Martyr*, a compound of exquisite beauties and absurdities of the most frantic description. The part of St. Catherine (very inappropriately allotted to Mrs. Eleanor Gwyn) is beautiful throughout, and that of Maximin is quite captivating in

its outrageousness.   The Astral spirits who appear gave
occasion for some terrible parody in the *Rehearsal*, but
their verses are in themselves rather attractive.   An
account of the final scene of the play will perhaps show
better than anything else the rant and folly in which
authors indulged, and which audiences applauded in these
plays.   The Emperor Maximin is dissatisfied with the
conduct of the upper powers in reference to his domestic
peace ; he thus expresses his dissatisfaction : —

> What had the gods to do with me or mine ?
> Did I molest your heaven ?
> Why should you then make Maximin your foe,
> Who paid you tribute, which he need not do ?
> Your altars I with smoke of rams did crown
> For which you leaned your hungry nostrils down,
> All daily gaping for my incense there,
> More than your sun could draw you in a year.
> And you for this these plagues have on me sent.
> But, by the gods (by Maximin I meant),
> Henceforth I and my world
> Hostility with you and yours declare.
> Look to it, gods ! for you the aggressors are,
> Keep you your rain and sunshine in your skies,
> And I'll keep back my flame and sacrifice.
> Your trade of heaven shall soon be at a stand
> And all your goods lie dead upon your hand.

Thereupon an aggrieved and possibly shocked follower,
of the name of Placidius, stabs him, but the Emperor wrests
the dagger from him and returns the blow.   Then follows
this stage direction : " Placidius falls and the Emperor
staggers after him and sits down upon him."   From this
singular throne his guards offer to assist him.   But he de-
clines help, and having risen once sits down again upon
Placidius, who, despite the stab and the weight of the
Emperor, is able to address an irreproachable decasyllabic

couplet to the audience. Thereupon Maximin again stabs
the person upon whom he is sitting, and they both expire
as follows :—

Plac. Oh! I am gone. *Max.* And after thee I go,
Revenging still and following ev'n to the other world my blow
And shoving back this earth on which I sit
I'll mount and scatter all the gods I hit.

                                    [*Stabs him again.*]

Tyrannic Love was followed by the two parts of *Almanzor and Almahide*, or the *Conquest of Granada*, the
triumph and at the same time the *reductio ad absur-
dum* of the style. I cannot do better than give a full
argument of this famous production, which nobody now
reads, and which is full of lines that everybody habitually
quotes.

The kingdom of Granada under its last monarch, Boabdelin, is divided by the quarrels of factions, or rather
families—the Abencerrages and the Zegrys. At a festival
held in the capital this dissension breaks out. A stranger
interferes on what appears to be the weaker side, and kills
a prominent leader of the opposite party, altogether dis-
regarding the king's injunctions to desist. He is seized
by the guards and ordered for execution, but is then
discovered to be Almanzor, a valiant person lately arrived
from Africa, who has rendered valuable assistance to the
Moors in their combat with the Spaniards. The king
thereupon apologizes, and Almanzor addresses much
outrageous language to the factions. This is successful,
and harmony is apparently restored. Then there enters
the Duke of Arcos, a Spanish envoy, who propounds hard
conditions ; but Almanzor remarks that " the Moors have
Heaven and me," and the duke retires. Almahide, the
king's betrothed, sends a messenger to invite him to a

dance ; but Almanzor insists upon a sally first, and the
first act ends with the acceptance of this order of amuse-
ment. The second opens with the triumphant return of
the Moors, the ever-victorious Almanzor having captured
the Duke of Arcos. Then is introduced the first female
character of importance, Lyndaraxa, sister of Zulema,
the Zegry chief, and representative throughout the drama
of the less amiable qualities of womankind. Abdalla,
the king's brother, makes love to her, and she very
plainly tells him that if he were king she might have
something to say to him. Zulema's factiousness strongly
seconds his sister's ambition and her jealousy of Almahide, and the act ends by the formation of a conspiracy
against Boabdelin, the conspirators resolving to attach
the invincible Almanzor to their side. The third act
borrows its opening from the incident of Hotspur's wrath,
Almanzor being provoked with Boabdelin for the same
cause as Harry Percy with Henry IV. Thus he is disposed to join Abdalla, while Abdelmelech, the chief of the
Abencerrages, is introduced in a scene full of " sighs and
flames," as the prince's rival for the hand of Lyndaraxa.
The promised dance takes place with one of Dryden's
delightful, and, alas, scarcely ever wholly quotable lyrics.
The first two stanzas may however be given :—

> Beneath a myrtle's shade,
> Which love for none but happy lovers made,
> I slept, and straight my love before me brought
> Phyllis, the object of my waking thought.
> Undressed she came my flame to meet,
> While love strewed flowers beneath her feet,
> Flowers which, so pressed by her, became more sweet.
>
> From the bright vision's head
> A careless veil of lawn was loosely shed,
> From her white temples fell her shaded hair,
> Like cloudy sunshine, not too brown nor fair.

> Her hands, her lips, did love inspire,
> Her every grace my heart did fire,
> But most her eyes, which languished with desire.

It is a thousand pities that the quotation cannot be continued; but it cannot, though the verse is more artfully beautiful even than here.

While, however, the king and his court are listening and looking, mischief is brewing. Almanzor, Abdalla, and the Zegrys are in arms. The king is driven in; Almahide is captured. Then a scene takes place between Almanzor and Almahide in the full spirit of the style. Almanzor sues for Almahide as a prisoner that he may set her at liberty; but a rival appears in the powerful Zulema. Almanzor is disobliged by Abdalla, and at once makes his way to the citadel, whither Boabdelin has fled, and offers him his services. At the beginning of the fourth act they are of course accepted with joy, and equally of course effectual. Almanzor renews his suit, but Almahide refers him to her father. The fifth act is still fuller of extravagances. Lyndaraxa holds a fort which has been committed to her against both parties, and they discourse with her from without the walls. The unlucky Almanzor prefers his suit to the king and to Almahide's father; has recourse to violence on being refused, and is overpowered —for a wonder—and bound. His life is however spared, and after a parting scene with Almahide he withdraws from the city.

The second part opens in the Spanish camp but soon shifts to Granada, where the unhappy Boabdelin has to face the mutinies provoked by the expulsion of Almanzor. The king has to stoop to entreat Almahide, now his queen, to use her influence with her lover to come back. An act of fine confused fighting follows, in which Lyndaraxa's castle is stormed, the stormers in their turn driven out by the Duke of Arcos and Abdalla, who has joined the Spaniards, and a general *imbroglio* created. But Almanzor obeys Almahide's summons with the result of more sighs and flames. The conduct of Almahide is unexceptionable, but Boabdelin's jealousy is inevitably aroused, and this in its turn mortally offends the queen, which again offends Almanzor. More inexplicable embroilment follows, and Lyndaraxa tries her charms vainly on the champion. The war once more centres round the Albayzin, Lyndaraxa's sometime fortress, and it is not flippant to say that every one fights with every one else ; after which the hero sees the ghost of his mother, and addresses it *more suo*. Yet another love-scene follows, and then Zulema, who has not forgotten his passion for Almahide, brings a false accusation against her, the assumed partner of her guilt being however not Almanzor but Abdelmelech. This leaves the hero free to undertake the wager of battle for his mistress, though he is distracted with jealous fear that Zulema's tale is true. The result of the ordeal is a foregone conclusion ; but Almahide, though her innocence is proved, is too angry with her husband for doubting her to forgive him, and solemnly forswears his society. She and Almanzor meet once more, and by this time even the conventionalities of the heroic play allow him to kiss her hand. The king is on the watch and breaks in with fresh accusations ; but the Spaniards at the gates cut short the discussion and (at last) the embroilment and suffering of true love. The catastrophe is arrived at in the most approved manner. Boabdelin dies fighting ; Lyndaraxa, who has given traitorous help with her Zegrys, is proclaimed queen by Ferdinand but almost immediately stabbed by Abdelmelech. Almanzor turns out to be the

E

long-lost son of the Duke of Arcos; and Almahide, encouraged by Queen Isabella, owns that when her year
of widowhood is up she may possibly be induced to
crown his flames.

Such is the barest outline of this famous play, and I fear
that as it is it is too long, though much has been omitted,
including the whole of a pleasing underplot of love between two very creditable lovers, Osmyn and Benzayda.
Its preposterous "revolutions and discoveries," the wild
bombast of Almanzor and others, the apparently purpose-
less embroilment of the action in ever-new turns and
twists are absurd enough. But there is a kind of generous
and noble spirit animating it which could not fail to catch
an audience blinded by fashion to its absurdities. There
is a skilful sequence even in the most preposterous events,
which must have kept up the interest unfalteringly; and
all over the dialogue are squandered and lavished flowers
of splendid verse. Many of its separate lines are, as
has been said, constantly quoted without the least idea
on the quoter's part of their origin, and many more are
quotable. Everybody, for instance, knows the vigorous
couplet :—

> Forgiveness to the injured does belong,
> But they ne'er pardon who have done the wrong;

but everybody does not know the preceding couplet, which
is perhaps better still :—

> A blush remains in a forgiven face,
> It wears the silent tokens of disgrace.

Almanzor's tribute to Lyndaraxa's beauty, at the same
time that he rejects her advances, is in little, perhaps, as
good an instance as could be given of the merits of the

poetry and of the stamp of its spirit, and with this I must be content :—

> Fair though you are
> As summer mornings, and your eyes more bright
> Than stars that twinkle on a winter's night ;
> Though you have eloquence to warm and move
> Cold age and fasting hermits into love ;
> Though Almahide with scorn rewards my care
> Yet than to change 'tis nobler to despair.
> My love's my soul and that from fate is free,
> 'Tis that unchanged and deathless part of me.

The audience that cheered this was not wholly vile.

The *Conquest of Granada* appeared in 1670, and in the following year the famous *Rehearsal* was brought out at the King's Theatre. The importance of this event in Dryden's life is considerable, but it has been somewhat exaggerated. In the first place, the satire, keen as much of it is, is only half directed against himself. The original Bayes was beyond all doubt Davenant, to whom some of the jokes directly apply, while they have no reference to Dryden. In the second place, the examples of heroic plays selected for parody and ridicule are by no means exclusively drawn from Dryden's theatre. His brothers-in-law, Edward and Robert Howard, and others figure beside him, and the central character is, on the whole, as composite as might be expected from the number of authors whose plays are satirized. Although fathered by Buckingham it seems likely that not much of the play is actually his. His coadjutors are said to have been Butler, Sprat, and Martin Clifford, Master of the Charterhouse, author of some singularly ill-tempered if not very pointed remarks on Dryden's plays, which were not published till long afterwards. Butler's hand is indeed traceable in many of

the parodies of heroic diction, none of which are so good
as his acknowledged "Dialogue of Cat and Puss." The
wit and, for the most part, the justice of the satire are
indisputable, and, if it be true, as I am told, that the
Rehearsal does not now make a good acting play, the fact
does not bear favourable testimony to the culture and re-
ceptive powers of modern audiences. But there were many
reasons why Dryden should take the satire very coolly, as
in fact he did. As he says, with his customary proud
humility, "his betters were much more concerned than
himself;" and it seems highly probable that Buckingham's
coadjutors, confiding in his good nature or his inability
to detect the liberty, had actually introduced not a few
traits of his own into this singularly composite portrait. In
the second place, the farce was what would be now called
an advertisement, and a very good one. Nothing can be a
greater mistake than to say or to think that the *Rehearsal*
killed heroic plays. It did nothing of the kind, Dryden
himself going on writing them for some years until his
own fancy made him cease, and others continuing still
longer. There is a play of Crowne's, *Caligula*, in which
many of the scenes are rhymed, dating as late as 1698,
and the general character of the heroic play, if not the
rhymed form, continued almost unaltered. Certainly
Dryden's equanimity was very little disturbed. Buckingham he paid off in kind long afterwards, and his Grace
immediately proceeded by his answer to show how little
he can have had to do with the *Rehearsal*. To Sprat and
Clifford no allusions that I know of are to be found in his
writings. As for Butler, an honourable mention in a letter to Lawrence Hyde shows how little acrimony he felt
towards him. Indeed, it may be said of Dryden that he was
at no time touchy about personal attacks. It was only when,

as Shadwell subsequently did, the assailants became outrageous in their abuse and outstepped the bounds of fair
literary warfare, or when, as in Blackmore's case, there
was some singular ineptitude in the fashion of the attack,
that he condescended to reply.

It is all the more surprising that he should, at no great
distance of time, have engaged gratuitously in a contest
which brought him no honour, and in which his allies
were quite unworthy of him.   Elkanah Settle was one of
Rochester's innumerable led-poets, and was too utterly be-
neath contempt to deserve even Rochester's spite.   The
character of Doeg, ten years later, did Settle complete justice.   He had a " blundering kind of melody " about him,
but absolutely nothing else.   However, a heroic play of
his, the *Empress of Morocco,* had considerable vogue for
some incomprehensible reason.   Dryden allowed himself to
be drawn by Crowne and Shadwell into writing with them
a pamphlet of criticisms on the piece.   Settle replied by a
study, as we should say nowadays, of the very vulnerable
Conquest of Granada.   This is the only instance in which
Dryden went out of his way to attack any one ; and even
in this instance Settle had given some cause by an allusion
of a contemptuous kind in his preface.   But as a rule the
laureate showed himself proof against much more veno-
mous criticisms than any that Elkanah was capable of.   It
is perhaps not uncharitable to suspect that the preface of
the *Empress of Morocco* bore to some extent the blame of
the *Rehearsal,* which it must be remembered was for years
amplified and re-edited with parodies of fresh plays of
Dryden's as they appeared.   If this were the case it would
not be the only instance of such a transference of irrita-
tion, and it would explain Dryden's otherwise inexplicable
conduct.   His attack on Settle is, from a strictly literary

point of view, one of his most unjustifiable acts. The
pamphlet, it is true, is said to have been mainly " Starch
Johnny " Crowne's, and the character of its strictures
is quite different from Dryden's broad and catholic manner of censuring. But the adage, " tell me with whom you
live," is peculiarly applicable in such a case, and Dryden
must be held reponsible for the assault, whether its
venom be really due to himself, to Crowne, or to the
foul-mouthed libeller of whose virulence the laureate
himself was in years to come to have but too familiar
experience.

A very different play in 1672 gave Dryden almost as much
credit in comedy as the *Conquest of Granada* in tragedy.
There is indeed a tragic or serious underplot (and a very
ridiculous one too) in *Marriage à la Mode*. But its main
interest, and certainly its main value, is comic. It is
Dryden's only original excursion into the realms of the
higher comedy. For his favourite pair of lovers he here
substitutes a quartette. Rhodophil and Doralice are a
fashionable married pair, who, without having actually
exhausted their mutual affection, are of opinion that
their character is quite gone if they continue faithful
to each other any longer. Rhodophil accordingly lays
siege to Melantha, a young lady who is intended, though
he does not know this, to marry his friend Palamede,
while Palamede, deeply distressed at the idea of matrimony, devotes himself to Doralice. The cross purposes
of this quartette are admirably related, and we are given to
understand that no harm comes of it all. But in Doralice
and Melantha, Dryden has given studies of womankind
quite out of his usual line. Melantha is, of course, far
below Millamant, but it is not certain that that delightful
creation of Congreve's genius does not owe something to

her. Doralice, on the other hand, has ideas as to the philosophy of flirtation which do her no little credit. It is a thousand pities that the play is written in the language of the time, which makes it impossible to revive and difficult to read without disgust.

Nothing of this kind can or need be said about the play which followed, the *Assignation*. It is vulgar, coarse, and dull; it was damned, and deserved it; while its successor *Amboyna*, is also deserving of the same epithets, though being a mere play of ephemeral interest, and serving its turn, it was not damned. The old story of the Amboyna massacre—a bad enough story certainly— was simply revived in order to excite the popular wrath against the Dutch.

The dramatic production which immediately succeeded these is one of the most curious of Dryden's performances. A disinclination to put himself to the trouble of designing a wholly original composition is among the most note-worthy of his literary characteristics. No man followed or copied in a more original manner, but it always seems to have been a relief to him to have something to follow or to copy. Two at least of his very best productions— *All for Love* and *Palamon and Arcite*—are specially remarkable in this respect. We can hardly say that the *State of Innocence* ranks with either of these; yet it has considerable merits—merits of which very few of those who repeat the story about "tagging Milton's verses" are aware. As for that story itself, it is not particularly creditable to the good manners of the elder poet. "Ay! young man, you may tag my verses if you will," is the traditional reply which Milton is said to have made to Dryden's request for permission to write the opera. The question of Dryden's relationship to Milton and his early opinion of *Paradise Lost* is rather a question for a Life of Milton than for the present pages : it is sufficient to say that, with his unfailing recognition of good work, Dryden undoubtedly appreciated Milton to the full long before Addison, as it is vulgarly held, taught the British public to admire him. As for the *State of Innocence* itself, the conception of such an opera has sometimes been derided as preposterous—a derision which seems to overlook the fact that Milton was himself, in some degree, indebted to an Italian dramatic original. The piece is not wholly in rhyme, but contains some very fine passages.

The time was approaching, however, when Dryden was to quit his "long-loved mistress Rhyme," as far as dramatic writing was concerned. These words occur in the prologue to *Aurengzebe*, which appeared in 1675. It would appear, indeed, that at this time Dryden was thinking of deserting not merely rhymed plays but play-writing altogether. The dedication to Mulgrave contains one of several allusions to his well-known plan of writing a great heroic poem. Sir George Mackenzie had recently put him upon the plan of reading through most of the earlier English poets, and he had done so attentively, with the result of aspiring to the epic itself. But he still continued to write dramas, though *Aurengzebe* was his last in rhyme, at least wholly in rhyme. It is in some respects a very noble play, free from the rants, the preposterous bustle, and the still more preposterous length of the *Conquest of Granada*, while possessing most of the merits of that singular work in an eminent degree. Even Dryden hardly ever went further in cunning of verse than in some of the passages of *Aurengzebe*, such as that well-known one which seems to take up an echo of *Macbeth* :—

When I consider life, 'tis all a cheat.
Yet, fooled with hope, men favour the deceit,
Trust on, and think to-morrow will repay.
To-morrow's falser than the former day,
Lies worse, and while it says, we shall be blest
With some new joys, cuts off what we possest.
Strange cozenage! none would live past years again
Yet all hope pleasure in what yet remain,
And from the dregs of life think to receive
What the first sprightly running could not give.
I'm tired with waiting for this chemic gold
Which fools us young and beggars us when old.

There is a good deal of moralizing of this melancholy
kind in the play, the characters of which are drawn with
a serious completeness not previously attempted by the
author. It is perhaps the only one of Dryden's which,
with very little alteration, might be acted, at least as a
curiosity, at the present day. It is remarkable that the
structure of the verse in the play itself would have led
to the conclusion that Dryden was about to abandon
rhyme. There is in *Aurengzebe* a great tendency towards
enjambement; and as soon as this tendency gets the upper
hand, a recurrence to blank verse is, in English dramatic
writing, tolerably certain. For the intonation of English
is not, like the intonation of French, such that rhyme is an
absolute necessity to distinguish verse from prose; and
where this necessity does not exist, rhyme must always
appear to an intelligent critic a more or less impertinent
intrusion in dramatic poetry. Indeed the main thing
which had for a time converted Dryden and others
to the use of the couplet in drama was a curious notion
that blank verse was too easy for long and dignified compositions. It was thought by others that the secret of it
had been lost, and that the choice was practically between

bad blank verse and good rhyme. In *All for Love*
Dryden very shortly showed, *ambulando*, that this notion
was wholly groundless. From this time forward he
was faithful to the model he had now adopted and—
which was of the greatest importance—he induced others to
be faithful too. Had it not been for this, it is almost certain
that *Venice Preserved* would have been in rhyme, that is to
say that it would have been spoilt. In this same year,
1675, a publisher, Bentley, (of whom Dryden afterwards
spoke with considerable bitterness) brought out a play called
The Mistaken Husband, which he stated to have been
revised, and to have had a scene added to it by Dryden.
Dryden, however, definitely disowned it, and I cannot
think that it is in any part his ; though it is fair to say
that some good judges, notably Mr. Swinburne, think
differently.[1] Nearly three years passed without anything
of Dryden's appearing, and at last, at the end of 1677, or
the beginning of 1678, appeared a play as much better
than *Aurengzebe* as *Aurengzebe* was better than its fore-

[1] The list of Dryden's spurious or doubtful works is not large
or important. But a note of Pepys, mentioning a play of Dryden
entitled *Ladies à la Mode* which was acted and damned in 1668
has puzzled the commentators. There is no trace of this *Ladies
à la Mode*. But Mr. E. W. Gosse has in his collection a play entitled
The Mall or *The Modish Lovers*, which he thinks may possibly be
the very "mean thing" of Pepys' scornful mention. The difference
of title is not fatal, for Samuel was not over accurate in such
matters. The play is anonymous, but the preface is signed J. D.
The date is 1674, and the printing is execrable, and evidently not
revised by the author, whoever he was. Notwithstanding this
the prologue, the epilogue, and a song contain some vigorous verse
and phrase sometimes not a little suggestive of Dryden. In the
entire absence of external evidence connecting him with it, the
question, though one of much interest, is perhaps not one to be
dealt with at any length here.

runners.   This was *All for Love*, his first drama, in blank
verse, and his "only play written for himself."   More
will be said later on the curious fancy which made him
tread in the very steps of Shakespeare.   It is sufficient
to say now that the attempt, apparently foredoomed to
hopeless failure, is, on the contrary, a great success.
Antony and Cleopatra and *All for Love*, when they are
contrasted, only show by the contrast the difference of
kind, not the difference of degree, between their writers.
The heroic conception has here, in all probability, as
favourable exposition given to it as it is capable of, and
it must be admitted that it makes a not unfavourable
show even without the "dull sweets of rhyme" to drug
the audience into good humour with it.   The famous
scene between Antony and Ventidius divides with the
equally famous scene in *Don Sebastian* between Sebastian
and Dorax the palm among Dryden's dramatic efforts.
But as a whole the play is, I think, superior to *Don
Sebastian*.   The blank verse, too, is particularly interesting, because it was almost its author's first attempt
at that *crux ;* and because, for at least thirty years, hardly
any tolerable blank verse—omitting of course Milton's—
had been written by any one.   The model is excellent,
and it speaks Dryden's unerring literary sense, that, fresh
as he was from the study of *Paradise Lost*, and great as
was his admiration for its author, he does not for a
moment attempt to confuse the epic and the tragic modes
of the style.   *All for Love* was, and deserved to be, successful.   The play which followed it, *Limberham*, was,
and deserved to be, damned.   It must be one of the most
astonishing things to any one who has not fully grasped
the weakness as well as the strength of Dryden's character, that the noble matter and manner of *Aurengzebe*

and *All for Love* should have been followed by this
filthy stuff.   As a play, it is by no means Dryden's worst
piece of work ; but, in all other respects, the less said about
it the better.   During the time of its production the author
collaborated with Lee in writing the tragedy of *Œdipus*,
in which both the friends are to be seen almost at their
best.   On Dryden's part, the lyric incantation scenes are
perhaps most noticeable, and Lee mingles throughout his
usual bombast with his usual splendid poetry.   If any one
thinks this expression hyperbolical, I shall only ask him
to read *Œdipus*, instead of taking the traditional witticisms
about Lee for gospel.   There is of course plenty of—

> Let gods meet gods and jostle in the dark,

and the other fantastic follies, into which " metaphysical'" poetry and " heroic " plays had seduced men of
talent, and sometimes of genius ; but these can be excused
when they lead to such a passage as that where Œdipus
cries,—

> Thou coward ! yet
> Art living ? canst not, wilt not find the road
> To the great palace of magnificent death,
> Though thousand ways lead to his thousand doors
> Which day and night are still unbarred for all.

Œdipus led to a quarrel with the players of the King's
Theatre, of the merits of which, as we only have a
one-sided statement, it is not easy to judge.   But Dryden
seems to have formed a connexion about this time with
the other or Duke's company, and by them (April, 1679)
a " potboiling " adaptation of *Troilus and Cressida* was
brought out, which might much better have been left
unattempted.   Two years afterwards appeared the last
play (leaving operas and the scenes contributed to the

Duke of Guise out of the question) that Dryden was to write for many years. This was *The Spanish Friar*, a popular piece, possessed of a good deal of merit, from the technical point of view of the play-wright, but which I think has been somewhat over-rated, as far as literary excellence is concerned. The principal character is no doubt amusing, but he is heavily indebted to Falstaff on the one hand and to Fletcher's Lopez on the other ; and he reminds the reader of both his ancestors in a way which cannot but be unfavourable to himself. The play is to me most interesting because of the light it throws on Dryden's grand characteristic, the consummate crafts-manship with which he could throw himself into the popular feeling of the hour. This "Protestant play" is perhaps his most notable achievement of the kind in drama, and it may be admitted that some other achieve-ments of the same kind are less creditable.

Allusion has more than once been made to the very high quality, from the literary point of view, of the songs which appear in nearly all the plays of this long list. They constitute Dryden's chief title to a high rank as a composer of strictly lyrical poetry ; and there are indeed few things which better illustrate the range of his genius than these exquisite snatches. At first sight, it would not seem by any means likely that a poet whose greatest triumphs were won in the fields of satire and of argu-mentative verse should succeed in such things. Ordinary lyric, especially of the graver and more elaborate kind, might not surprise us from such a man. But the song-gift is something distinct from the faculty of ordinary lyrical composition ; and there is certainly nothing which necessarily infers it in the pointed declamation and close-ranked argument with which the name of Dryden is

oftenest associated.   But the later seventeenth century had
a singular gift for such performance—a kind of swan-song,
it might be thought, before the death-like slumber which,
with few and brief intervals, was to rest upon the English
lyric for a hundred years.   Dorset, Rochester, even Mulgrave, wrote singularly fascinating songs, as smooth and
easy as Moore's, and with far less of the commonplace and
vulgar about them.   Aphra Behn was an admirable, and
Tom Durfey a far from despicable, songster.   Even among
the common run of play-wrights, who have left no lyrical
and not much literary reputation, scraps and snatches with
which have the true song stamp are not unfrequently to
be found.   But Dryden excelled them all in the variety
of his cadences and the ring of his lines.   Nowhere do
we feel more keenly the misfortune of his licence of
language, which prevents too many of these charming
songs from being now quoted or sung.   Their abundance
may be illustrated by the fact that a single play, *The
Mock Astrologer*, contains no less than four songs of
the very first lyrical merit.   " You charmed me not with
that fair face," is an instance of the well-known common
measure which is so specially English, and which is poetry
or doggrel according to its cadence.   " After the pangs of
a desperate lover " is one of the rare examples of a real
dactylic metre in English, where the dactyls are not, as
usual, equally to be scanned as anapæsts.   " Calm was
the even, and clear was the sky," is a perfect instance of
what may be called archness in song ; and " Celimena
of my heart," though not much can be said for the matter
of it, is at least as much a metrical triumph as any of the
others.   Nor are the other plays less rich in similar work.
The song beginning " Farewell, ungrateful traitor," gives
a perfect example of a metre which has been used more

than once in our own days with great success; and
" Long between Love and Fear Phyllis tormented,"
which occurs in *The Assignation*, gives yet another example of the singular fertility with which Dryden devised
and managed measures suitable for song.   His lyrical
faculty impelled him also—especially in his early plays—
to luxuriate in incantation scenes, lyrical dialogues, and
so forth.   These have been ridiculed, not altogether unjustly, in *The Rehearsal ;* but the incantation scene in
Œdipus is very far above the average of such things; and
of not a few passages in *King Arthur* at least as much may
be said.

Dryden's energy was so entirely occupied with play-
writing during this period that he had hardly, it would
appear, time or desire to undertake any other work.
Towards the middle of it, however, when he had, by
poems and plays, already established himself as the
greatest living poet—Milton being out of the question—
he began to be asked for prologues and epilogues by
other poets, or by the actors on the occasion of the
revival of old plays.   These prologues and epilogues have
often been commented upon as one of the most curious
literary phenomena of the time.   The custom is still, on
special occasions, sparingly kept up on the stage ; but the
prologue, and still more the epilogue, to the Westminster
play are the chief living representatives of it.   It was usual
to comment in these pieces on circumstances of the day,
political and other.   It was also usual to make personal
appeals to the audience for favour and support very much
in the manner of the old Trouvères when they commended
their wares.   But more than all, and worst of all, it was
usual to indulge in the extremest licence both of language
and meaning.   The famous epilogue—one of Dryden's

own—to *Tyrannic Love*, in which Mrs. Eleanor Gwyn,
being left for dead on the stage, in the character of
St. Catharine, and being about to be carried out by the
scene-shifters, exclaims,—

> Hold! are you mad? you damned confounded dog,
> I am to rise and speak the epilogue,

is only a very mild sample of these licences, upon which
Macaulay has commented with a severity which is for
once absolutely justifiable. There was, however, no poet
who had the knack of telling allusion to passing events as
Dryden had, and he was early engaged as a prologue writer.
The first composition that we have of this kind written
for a play not his own is the prologue to *Albumazar*, a
curious piece, believed, but not known to have been written
by a certain Tomkis in James the First's reign, and rank-
ing among the many which have been attributed with
more or less (generally less) show of reason to Shakespeare.
Dryden's knowledge of the early English drama was not
exhaustive, and he here makes a charge of plagiarism
against Ben Jonson, for which there is in all probability
not the least ground. The piece contains, however, as
do most of these vigorous, though unequal compositions,
many fine lines. The next production of the kind not
intended for a play of his own is the prologue to the first
performance of the king's servants, after they had been
burnt out of their theatre, and this is followed by many
others. In 1673 a prologue to the University of Oxford,
spoken when the *Silent Woman* was acted, is the first of
many of the same kind. It has been mentioned that
Dryden speaks slightingly of these University prologues,
but they are among his best pieces of the class, and are for
the most part entirely free from the ribaldry with which

he was but too often wont to alloy them. In these years
pieces intended to accompany Carlell's *Arviragus and Phi-
licia*, Etherege's *Man of Mode*, Charles Davenant's *Circe*,
Lee's *Mithridates*, Shadwell's *True Widow*, Lee's *Cæsar
Borgia*, Tate's *Loyal General*, and not a few others occur.
A specimen of the style in which Dryden excelled so remarkably, and which is in itself so utterly dead, may
fairly be given here, and nothing can be better for the
purpose than the most famous prologue to the University
of Oxford. This is the prologue in which the poet at
once displays his exquisite capacity for flattery, his command over versification, and his singular antipathy to his
own Alma Mater; an antipathy which it may be pointed
out is confirmed by the fact of his seeking his master's
degree rather at Lambeth than at Cambridge. Whether
any solution to the enigma can be found in Dennis's remark
that the "younger fry" at Cambridge preferred Settle to
their own champion, it would be vain to attempt to
determine. The following piece, however, may be taken
as a fair specimen of the more decent prologue of the later
seventeenth century:—

> Though actors cannot much of learning boast,
> Of all who want it, we admire it most:
> We love the praises of a learned pit,
> As we remotely are allied to wit.
> We speak our poet's wit, and trade in ore,
> Like those, who touch upon the golden shore;
> Betwixt our judges can distinction make,
> Discern how much, and why, our poems take;
> Mark if the fools, or men of sense, rejoice;
> Whether the applause be only sound or voice.
> When our fop gallants, or our city folly,
> Clap over-loud, it makes us melancholy:
> We doubt that scene which does their wonder raise,
> And, for their ignorance, contemn their praise.

Judge, then, if we who act, and they who write,
Should not be proud of giving you delight.
London likes grossly ; but this nicer pit
Examines, fathoms all the depths of wit ;
The ready finger lays on every blot ;
Knows what should justly please, and what should not.
Nature, herself lies open to your view,
You judge, by her, what draught of her is true,
Where outlines false, and colours seem too faint,
Where bunglers daub, and where true poets paint.
But by the sacred genius of this place,
By every Muse, by each domestic grace,
Be kind to wit, which but endeavours well,
And, where you judge, presumes not to excel.
Our poets hither for adoption come,
As nations sued to be made free of Rome ;
Not in the suffragating tribes to stand,
But in your utmost, last, provincial band.
If his ambition may those hopes pursue,
Who with religion loves your arts and you,
Oxford to him a dearer name shall be,
Than his own mother-university.
Thebes did his green, unknowing, youth engage ;
He chooses Athens in his riper age.

During this busy period, Dryden's domestic life had been
comparatively uneventful. His eldest son had been born
either in 1665 or in 1666, it seems not clear which. His
second son, John, was born a year or two later, and the
third, Erasmus Henry, in May, 1669. These three sons
were all the children Lady Elizabeth brought him. The two
eldest went, like their father, to Westminster, and had their
schoolboy troubles there, as letters of Dryden still extant
show. During the whole period, except in his brief visits to
friends and patrons in the country, he was established in
the house in Gerrard Street, which is identified with his
name.[1] While his children were young, his means must

[1] A house in Fetter Lane, now divided into two, bears a

have been sufficient, and, for those days, considerable.
With his patrimony included, Malone has calculated that
for great part of the time his income must have
been fully 700*l.* a year, equal in purchasing power to
2000*l.* a year in Malone's time, and probably to nearer
3000*l.* now.   In June, 1668, the degree of Master of Arts,
to which, for some reason or other, Dryden had never proceeded at Cambridge, was, at the recommendation of the
king, conferred upon him by the Archbishop of Canterbury.
Two years later, in the summer of 1670, he was made
poet laureate and historiographer royal.[2] Davenant, the last
holder of the laureateship, had died two years previously,
and Howell, the well-known author of the *Epistolæ Ho-
Elianæ*, and the late holder of the historiographership,
four years before.   When the two appointments were conferred on Dryden, the salary was fixed in the patent at
200*l.* a year, besides the butt of sack which the
economical James afterwards cut off, and arrears since
Davenant's death were to be paid.   In the same year, 1670
the death of his mother increased his income by the,
20*l.* a year which had been payable to him from the
Northamptonshire property.   From 1667, or thereabouts,
Dryden had been in possession of a valuable partnership

plate stating that Dryden lived there. The plate, as I was informed by the present occupiers, replaces a stone slab or inscription which was destroyed in some alterations not very many
years ago. I know of no reference to this house in any book,
nor does Mr. J. C. Collins, who called my attention to it. If
Dryden ever lived here, it must have been between his residence
with Herringman and his marriage.

  [2] The patent, given by Malone, is dated Aug. 18.   Mr. W.
Noel Sainsbury, of the Record Office, has pointed out to me a
preliminary warrant to "our Attorney or Solicitor Generall" to
"prepare a Bill" for the purpose dated April 13.

with the players of the king's house, for whom he con-
tracted to write three plays a year in consideration of a
share and a quarter of the profits.   Dryden's part of the
contract was not performed, it seems, but the actors declare
that at any rate for some years their part was, and that
the poet's receipts averaged from 300*l.* to 400*l.* a year,
besides which he had (sometimes at any rate) the third
night, and (we may suppose always) the bookseller's fee for
the copyright of the printed play, which together averaged
100*l.* a play or more.   Lastly, at the extreme end of
the period most probably, but certainly before 1679, the
king granted him an additional pension of 100*l.* a year.
The importance of this pension is more than merely
pecuniary, for this is the grant, the confirmation of which
after some delay by James, was taken by Macaulay as
the wages of apostasy.

The pecuniary prosperity of this time was accompanied
by a corresponding abundance of the good things which
generally go with wealth.   Dryden was familiar with most
of the literary nobles and gentlemen of Charles's court,
and Dorset, Etherege, Mulgrave, Sedley, and Rochester
were among his special intimates or patrons, whichever
word may be preferred.   The somewhat questionable boast
which he made of this familiarity Nemesis was not long
in punishing, and the instrument which Nemesis chose was
Rochester himself.   It might be said of this famous person,
whom Etherege has hit off so admirably in his Dorimant,
that he was, except in intellect, the worst of all the courtiers
of the time, because he was one of the most radically un-
amiable.   It was truer of him even than of Pope, that he
was sure to play some monkey trick or other on those who
were unfortunate enough to be his intimates.   He had
relations with most of the literary men of his time, but

those relations almost always ended badly. Sometimes he set
them at each other like dogs, or procured for one some
court favour certain to annoy a rival; sometimes he
satirized them coarsely in his foul-mouthed poems; sometimes, as we shall see, he forestalled the Chevalier de
Rohan in his method of repartee. As early as 1675
Rochester had disobliged Dryden, though the exact
amount of the injury has certainly been exaggerated by
Malone, whom most biographers, except Mr. Christie, have
followed. There is little doubt (though Mr. Christie thinks
otherwise) that one of the chief functions of the poet
laureate was to compose masques and such like pieces to
be acted by the court; indeed, this appears to have been
the main regular duty of the office at least in the seventeenth century. That Crowne should have been charged
with the composition of *Calisto* was therefore a slight to
Dryden. Crowne was not a bad play-wright. He might
perhaps by a plagiarism from Lamb's criticism on Heywood
be called a kind of prose Dryden, and a characteristic
saying of Dryden's, which has been handed down, seems
to show that the latter recognized the fact. But the
addition to the charge against Rochester that he afterwards interfered to prevent an epilogue, which Dryden
wrote for Crowne's piece, from being recited, rests
upon absolutely no authority, and it is not even certain
that the epilogue referred to was actually written by
Dryden.

In the year 1679, however, Dryden had a much more
serious taste of Rochester's malevolence. He had recently
become very intimate with Lord Mulgrave, who had
quarrelled with Rochester. Personal courage was not
Rochester's forte, and he had shown the white feather
when challenged by Mulgrave. Shortly afterwards there

was circulated in manuscript an *Essay on Satire*, containing virulent attacks on the king, on Rochester and the Duchesses of Cleveland and Portsmouth. How any one could ever have suspected that the poem was Dryden's it is difficult to understand. To begin with, he never at any time in his career lent himself as a hired literary bravo to any private person. In the second place, that he should attack the king from whom he derived the greatest part of his income, was inconceivable. Thirdly, no literary judge could for one moment connect him with the shambling doggrel lines which distinguish the *Essay on Satire* in its original form. A very few couplets have some faint ring of Dryden's verse, but not more than is perceivable in the work of many other poets and poetasters of the time. Lastly, Mulgrave, who, with some bad qualities, was truthful and fearless enough, expressly absolves Dryden as being not only innocent, but ignorant of the whole matter. However, Rochester chose to identify him as the author, and in letters still extant almost expressly states his belief in the fact, and threatens to " leave the repartee to Black Will with a cudgel." On the 18th December, as Dryden was going home at night, through Rose Alley, Covent Garden, he was attacked and beaten by masked men. Fifty pounds reward (deposited at what is now called Childs' Bank) was offered for the discovery of the offenders, and afterwards a pardon was promised to the actual criminals if they would divulge the name of their employer, but nothing came of it. The intelligent critics of the time affected to consider the matter a disgrace to Dryden, and few of the subsequent attacks on him fail to notice it triumphantly. How frequent those attacks soon became the next chapter will show.

CHAPTER IV.

SATIRICAL AND DIDACTIC POEMS.

In the year 1680 a remarkable change came over the character of Dryden's work. Had he died in this year (and
he had already reached an age at which many men's work is
done) he would not at the present time rank very high even
among the second class of English poets. In pure poetry
he had published nothing of the slightest consequence for
fourteen years, and though there was much admirable
work in his dramas, they could as wholes only be praised
by allowance. Of late years, too, he had given up the
style—rhymed heroic drama—which he had specially
made his own. He had been for some time casting
about for an opportunity of again taking up strictly
poetical work ; and as usually happens with the favourites
of fortune, a better opportunity than any he could have
elaborated for himself was soon presented to him. The
epic poem which, as he tells us, he intended to write, would
doubtless have contained many fine passages and much
splendid versification ; but it almost certainly would not
have been the best thing in its kind even in its own language. The series of satirical and didactic poems which,
in the space of less than seven years he was now to produce, occupies the position which the epic would almost
to a certainty have failed to attain. Not only is there

nothing better of their own kind in English, but it may almost be said that there is nothing better in any other literary language.   Satire, argument, and exposition may possibly be half-spurious kinds of poetry—that is a question which need not be argued here.   But among satirical and didactic poems *Absalom and Achitophel, The Medal, Mac-flecknoe, Religio Laici, The Hind and the Panther*, hold the first place in company with very few rivals.   In a certain kind of satire to be defined presently they have no rival at all ; and in a certain kind of argumentative exposition they have no rival except in Lucretius.

It is probable that, until he was far advanced in middle life, Dryden had paid but little attention to political and religious controversies, though he was well enough versed in their terms, and had a logical and almost scholastic mind.   I have already endeavoured to show the unlikeli-ness of his ever having been a very fervent Roundhead, and I do not think that there is much more probability of his having been a very fervent Royalist.   His literary work, his few friendships, and the tavern-coffeehouse life which took up so much of the time of the men of that day, probably occupied him sufficiently in the days of his earlier manhood.   He was loyal enough, no doubt, not merely in lip-loyalty, and was perfectly ready to furnish an *Amboyna* or anything else that was wanted ; but for the first eighteen years of Charles the Second's reign, the nation at large felt little interest, of the active kind, in political questions. Dryden almost always reflected the sympathies of the nation at large.   The Popish Plot, however, and the dangerous excitement which the misgovernment of Charles on the one hand and the machinations of Shaftes-bury on the other produced, found him at an age when seri-ous subjects are at any rate by courtesy supposed to possess

greater attractions than they exert in youth. Tradition
has it that he was more or less directly encouraged by
Charles to write one, if not two, of the poems which in a
few months made him the first satirist in Europe. It is
possible, for Charles had a real if not a very lively interest
in literature, was a sound enough critic in his way, and
had ample shrewdness to perceive the advantage to his
own cause which he might gain by enlisting Dryden.
However this may be, *Absalom and Achitophel* was published about the middle of November, 1681, a week or so
before the grand jury threw out the bill against Shaftesbury on a charge of high treason. At no time before,
and hardly at any time since, did party-spirit run higher,
and though the immediate object of the poem was de-
feated by the fidelity of the brisk boys of the city to
their leader, there is no question that the poem worked
powerfully among the influences which after the most
desperate struggle, short of open warfare, in which any
English sovereign has ever been engaged, finally won for
Charles the victory over the Exclusionists, by means at
least ostensibly constitutional and legitimate. It is, however, with the literary rather than with the political aspect
of the matter that we are here concerned.

The story of Absalom and Achitophel has obvious capacities for political adaptation, and it had been more than
once so used in the course of the century, indeed (it would
appear), in the course of the actual political struggle in
which Dryden now engaged. Like many other of the
greatest writers, Dryden was wont to carry out Molière's
principle to the fullest, and to care very little for technical
originality of plan or main idea. The form which his
poem took was also in many ways suggested by the prevailing literary tastes of the day. Both in France and in

England the character or portrait, a set description of a given person in prose or verse, had for some time been fashionable. Clarendon in the one country, Saint Evremond in the other, had in particular composed prose portraits which have never been surpassed. Dryden accordingly made his poem little more than a string of such portraits, connected together by the very slenderest thread of narrative, and interspersed with occasional speeches in which the arguments of his own side were put in a light as favourable, and those of the other in a light as unfavourable as possible. He was always very careless of anything like a regular plot for his poems—a carelessness rather surprising in a practised writer for the stage. But he was probably right in neglecting this point. The subjects with which he dealt were of too vital an interest to his readers to allow them to stay and ask the question, whether the poems had a beginning, a middle, and an end. Sharp personal satire and biting political denunciation needed no such setting as this, a setting which to all appearance Dryden was as unable as he was unwilling to give. He could, however, and did give other things of much greater importance. The wonderful command over the couplet of which he had displayed the beginnings in his early poems, and which had in twenty years of play-writing been exercised and developed, till its owner was in as thorough training as a professional athlete, was the first of these. The second was a faculty of satire, properly so called, which was entirely novel. The third was a faculty of specious argument in verse which, as has been said, no one save Lucretius has ever equalled, and which, if it falls short of the great Roman's in logical exactitude, hardly falls short of it in poetical ornament, and excels it in a sort of triumphant vivacity which hurries the

reader along, whether he will or no.   All these three gifts
are almost indifferently exemplified in the series of poems
now under discussion, and each of them may deserve a little
consideration before we proceed to give account of the
poems themselves.

The versification of English satire before Dryden had
been almost without exception harsh and rugged.   There
are whole passages of Marston and of Donne, as well as
more rarely of Hall, which can only be recognized for verse
by the rattle of the rhymes and by a diligent scansion with
the finger.   Something the same, allowing for the influence of Waller and his school, may be said of Marvell and
even of Oldham.   Meanwhile the octosyllabic satire of
Cleveland, Butler and others, though less violently uncouth
than the decasyllables, was purposely grotesque.   There is
some difference of opinion as to how far the heroic satirists
themselves were intentionally rugged.   Donne, when he
chose, could write with perfect sweetness, and Marston
could be smooth enough in blank verse.   It has been
thought that some mistaken classical tradition made the
early satirists adopt their jaw-breaking style, and there
may be something to be said for this.   But I think that
regard must, in fairness, also be had to the very imperfect
command of the couplet which they possessed.   The languid
cadence of its then ordinary form was unsuited for satire,
and the satirists had not the art of quickening and varying it.   Hence the only resource was to make it as like
prose as possible.   But Dryden was in no such case.   His
native gifts and his enormous practice in play-writing had
made the couplet as natural a vehicle to him for any form
of discourse as blank verse or as plain prose.   The form of
it too, which he had most affected, was specially suited for
satire.   In the first place this form had, as has already

been noted, a remarkably varied cadence ; in the second, its strong antitheses and smart telling hits lent themselves to personal description and attack with consummate ease. There are passages of Dryden's satires in which every couplet has not only the force but the actual sound of a slap in the face. The rapidity of movement from one couplet to the other is another remarkable characteristic. Even Pope, master as he was of verse, often fell into the fault of isolating his couplets too much, as if he expected applause between each, and wished to give time for it. Dryden's verse on the other hand strides along with a careless Olympian motion, as if the writer were looking at his victims rather with a kind of good-humoured scorn than with any elaborate triumph.

This last remark leads us naturally to the second head, the peculiar character of Dryden's satire itself. In this respect it is at least as much distinguished from its predecessors as in the former. There had been a continuous tradition among satirists that they must affect immense moral indignation at the evils they attacked. Juvenal and still more Persius are probably responsible for this, and even Dryden's example did not put an end to the practice, for in the next century it is found in persons upon whom it sits with singular awkwardness, such as Churchill and Lloyd. Now this moral indignation, apt to be rather tiresome when the subject is purely ethical—Marston is a glaring example of this—becomes quite intolerable when the subject is political. It never does for the political satirist to lose his temper and to rave and rant and denounce with the air of an inspired prophet. Dryden, and perhaps Dryden alone, has observed this rule. As I have just observed, his manner towards his subjects is that of a cool and not ill-humoured scorn. They are great scoundrels certainly, but

they are probably even more contemptible than they are
vicious.   The well-known line—

They got a villain and we lost a fool,

expresses this attitude admirably, and the attitude in its
turn explains the frantic rage which Dryden's satire produced in his opponents.   There is yet another peculiarity
of this satire in which it stands almost alone.   Most satirists
are usually prone to the error of attacking either mere
types, or else individuals too definitely marked as individuals.   The first is the fault of Regnier and all the minor
French satirists, the second is the fault of Pope.   In the first
case the point and zest of the thing are apt to be lost, and
the satire becomes a declamation against vice and folly in
the abstract.   In the second case a suspicion of personal
pique comes in, and it is felt that the requirement of art,
the disengagement of the general law from the individual
instance, is not sufficiently attended to.   Regnier perhaps
only in Macette, Pope perhaps only in Atticus, escape this
Scylla and this Charybdis.   But Dryden rarely or never
falls into either's grasp.   His figures are always at once
types and individuals.   Zimri is at once Buckingham and
the idle grand seigneur who plays at politics and at learning, Achitophel at once Shaftesbury and the abstract
intriguer, Shimei at once Bethel and the sectarian politi-
cian of all days.   It is to be noticed also that in drawing
these satirical portraits, the poet has exercised a singular
judgment in selecting his traits.   If *Absalom and Achitophel* be compared with the replies it called forth, this is
especially noticeable.   Shadwell, for instance, in the almost
incredibly scurrilous libel which he put forth in answer to
the *Medal*, accuses Dryden of certain definite misdoings

and mis-sayings most of which are unbelievable while
others are inconclusive. Dryden on the other hand in the
character of Og confines himself in the adroitest way to
generalities. These generalities are not only much more
effective, but also much more difficult of disproval. When,
to recur to the already quoted and typical line attacking
the unlucky Johnson, Dryden says—

> They got a villain, and we lost a fool,

it is obviously useless for the person assailed to sit down
and write a rejoinder tending to prove that he is neither
one nor the other. He might clear himself from the charge
of villainy, but only at the inevitable cost of establishing
that of folly. But when Shadwell, in unquotable verses,
says to Dryden, on this or that day you did such and such
a discreditable thing, the reply is obvious. In the first place
the charge can be disproved, in the second it can be dis-
dained. When Dryden himself makes such charges it is
always in a casual and allusive way, as if there were no
general dissent as to the truth of his allegation, while he
takes care to be specially happy in his language. The disgraceful insinuation against Forbes, the famous if irreve-
rent dismissal of Lord Howard of Escrick—

> And canting Nadab let oblivion damn,
> Who made new porridge for the paschal lamb,

justify themselves by their form if not by their matter.
It has also to be noted that Dryden's facts are rarely dis-
putable. The famous passage in which Settle and Shadwell are yoked in a sentence of discriminating damnation
is an admirable example of this. It is absolutely true that
Settle had a certain faculty of writing, though the matter

of his verse was worthless ; and it is absolutely true that
Shadwell wrote worse, and was in some respects a duller
man, than any person of equal talents placed among English
men of letters.   There could not possibly be a more complete justification of *Macflecknoe* than the victim's complaint that "he had been represented as an Irishman,
though Dryden knew perfectly well that he had only once
been in Ireland, and that was but for a few hours."

Lastly has to be noticed Dryden's singular faculty of
verse argument.   He was, of course, by no means the first
didactic poet of talent in England.   Sir John Davies is
usually mentioned specially as his forerunner, and there
were others who would deserve notice in a critical history
of English poetry.   But Dryden's didactic poems are quite
unlike anything which came before them, and have never
been approached by anything that has come after them.
Doubtless they prove nothing ; indeed, the chief of them,
The Hind and the Panther, is so entirely desultory that it
could not prove anything ; but at the same time they have
a remarkable air of proving something.   Dryden had, in
reality, a considerable touch of the scholastic in his mind.
He delights at all times in the formulas of the schools,
and his various literary criticisms are frequently very fair
specimens of deductive reasoning.   The bent of his mind,
moreover, was of that peculiar kind which delights in
arguing a point.   Something of this may be traced in the
singular variety, not to say inconsistency, even of his
literary judgments.   He sees, for the time being, only the
point which he has set himself to prove, and is quite careless of the fact that he has proved something very different
yesterday, and is very likely to prove something different
still to-morrow.   But for the purposes of didactic poetry
he had special equipments unconnected with his merely

logical power. He was at all times singularly happy and
fertile in the art of illustration, and of concealing the
weakness of an argument in the most convincing way, by
a happy simile or jest. He steered clear of the rock on
which Lucretius has more than once gone nigh to split—
the repetition of dry formulas and professional terms. In
the *Hind and Panther*, indeed, the argument is, in great
part, composed of narrative and satirical portraiture. The
Fable of the Pigeons, the Character of the Buzzard, and a
dozen more such things, certainly prove as little as the
most determined enemy of the *belles lettres* could wish.
But *Religio Laici*, which is our best English didactic
poem, is not open to this charge, and is really a very good
piece of argument. Weaknesses here and there are, of
course, adroitly patched over with ornament, but still the
whole possesses a very fair capacity of holding water.
Here, too, the peculiar character of Dryden's poetic style
served him well. He speaks with surely affected depreciation of the style of the *Religio* as "unpolished and
rugged." In reality it is a model of the plainer sort of
verse, and nearer to his own admirable prose than anything else that can be cited.

One thing more, and a thing of the greatest importance,
has to be said about Dryden's satirical poems. There
never perhaps was a satirist who less abused his power for
personal ends. He only attacked Settle and Shadwell after
both had assailed him in the most virulent and unpro-
voked fashion. Many of the minor assailants whom, as we
shall see, *Absalom and Achitophel* raised up against him,
he did not so much as notice. On the other hand no kind
of personal grudge can be traced in many of his most
famous passages. The character of Zimri was not only perfectly true and just, but was also a fair literary tit-for-tat

in return for the *Rehearsal ;* nor did Buckingham's foolish rejoinder provoke the poet to say another word. Last of all, in no part of his satires is there the slightest reflection on Rochester, notwithstanding the disgraceful conduct of which he had been guilty. Rochester was dead, leaving no heirs and very few friends, so that at any time during the twenty years which Dryden survived him satirical allusion would have been safe and easy. But Dryden was far too manly to war with the dead, and far too manly even to indulge, as his great follower did, in vicious flings at the living.

Absalom and Achitophel is perhaps, with the exception of the St. Cecilia ode, the best known of all Dryden's poems to modern readers, and there is no need to give any very lengthy account of it, or of the extraordinary skill with which Monmouth is treated. The sketch, even now about the best existing in prose or verse, of the Popish Plot, the character and speeches of Achitophel, the unapproached portrait of Zimri, and the final harangue of David, have for generations found their places in every book of elegant extracts, either for general or school use. But perhaps the most characteristic passage of the whole, as indicating the kind of satire which Dryden now introduced for the first time, is the passage descriptive of Shimei—Slingsby Bethel —the Republican sheriff of the city :—

> But he, though bad, is followed by a worse,
> The wretch, who heaven's anointed dared to curse ;
> Shimei—whose youth did early promise bring
> Of zeal to God, and hatred to his King—
> Did wisely from expensive sins refrain,
> And never broke the sabbath but for gain :
> Nor ever was he known an oath to vent,
> Or curse, unless against the government.

G

Thus heaping wealth, by the most ready way
Among the Jews, which was to cheat and pray ;
The City, to reward his pious hate
Against his master, chose him magistrate.
His hand a vare of justice did uphold,
His neck was loaded with a chain of gold.
During his office treason was no crime,
The sons of Belial had a glorious time :
For Shimei, though not prodigal of pelf,
Yet loved his wicked neighbour as himself.
When two or three were gathered to declaim
Against the monarch of Jerusalem,
Shimei was always in the midst of them :
And, if they cursed the King when he was by,
Would rather curse than break good company.
If any durst his factious friends accuse,
He packed a jury of dissenting Jews ;
Whose fellow-feeling in the godly cause
Would free the suffering saint from human laws :
For laws are only made to punish those
Who serve the king, and to protect his foes.
If any leisure time he had from power,
Because 'tis sin to misemploy an hour,
His business was, by writing to persuade,
That kings were useless, and a clog to trade :
And that his noble style he might refine,
No Rechabite more shunned the fumes of wine.
Chaste were his cellars, and his shrieval board
The grossness of a city feast abhorred :
His cooks with long disuse their trade forgot ;
Cool was his kitchen, though his brains were hot.
Such frugal virtue malice may accuse,
But sure 'twas necessary to the Jews :
For towns, once burnt, such magistrates require,
As dare not tempt God's providence by fire.
With spiritual food he fed his servants well,
But free from flesh, that made the Jews rebel :
And Moses' laws he held in more account,
For forty days of fasting in the mount.

There had been nothing in the least like this before.

The prodigality of irony, the. sting in the tail of every couplet, the ingenuity by which the odious charges are made against the victim in the very words almost of the phrases which his party were accustomed to employ, and above all the polish of the language and the verse, and the tone of half-condescending banter, were things of which that time had no experience. The satire was as bitter as Butler's but less grotesque and less laboured.

It was not likely that at a time when pamphlet-writing was the chief employment of professional authors, and when the public mind was in the hottest state of excitement, such an onslaught as *Absalom and Achitophel* should remain unanswered. In three weeks from its appearance a parody, entitled *Towser the Second*, attacking Dryden, was published, the author of which is said to have been Henry Care. A few days later Buckingham proved, with tolerable convincingness, how small had been his own share in the *Rehearsal*, by putting forth some *Poetical Reflections* of the dreariest kind. Him followed an anonymous Nonconformist with *A Whip for the Fool's Back*, a performance which exposed his own back to a much more serious flagellation in the preface to the *Medal*. Next came Samuel Pordage's *Azaria and Hushai*. This work of "Lame Mephibosheth, the wizard's son," is weak enough in other respects, but shows that Dryden had already taught several of his enemies how to write. Lastly, Settle published *Absalom Senior*, perhaps the worst of all the replies, though containing evidences of its author's faculty for "rhyming and rattling." Of these and of subsequent replies Scott has given ample selections, ample, that is to say, for the general reader. But the student of Dryden can hardly appreciate his author fully, or estimate the debt which the English language owes to him unless he has read at least some of them in full.

The popularity of *Absalom and Achitophel* was immense and its sale rapid ; but the main object, the overthrowing of Shaftesbury, was not accomplished, and a certain triumph was even gained for that turbulent leader by the failure of the prosecution against him. This failure was celebrated by the striking of a medal with the legend *Laetamur*. Thereupon Dryden wrote the *Medal*. A very precise but probably apocryphal story is told by Spence of its origin. Charles, he says, was walking with Dryden in the Mall, and said to him, " If I were a poet, and I think I am poor enough to be one, I would write a poem on such a subject in such a manner," giving him at the same time hints for the *Medal*, which, when finished, was rewarded with a hundred broad pieces. The last part of the story is not very credible, for the king was not extravagant towards literature. The first is unlikely, because he was, in the first place, too much of a gentleman to reproach a man to whom he was speaking with the poverty of his profession ; and, in the second, too shrewd not to see that he laid himself open to a damaging repartee. However, the story is not impossible, and that is all that can be said of it. The *Medal* came out in March, 1682. It is a much shorter and a much graver poem than *Absalom and Achitophel*, extending to little more than 300 lines, and containing none of the picturesque personalities which had adorned its predecessor. Part of it is a bitter invective against Shaftesbury, part an argument as to the unfitness of republican institutions for England, and the rest an " Address to the Whigs," as the prose preface is almost exclusively. The language of the poem is nervous, its versification less lively than that of *Ab-*

salom and Achitophel, but not less careful. It is noticeable, too, that the *Medal* contains a line of fourteen syllables,

> Thou leap'st o'er all eternal truths in thy Pindaric way.

The Alexandrine was already a favourite device of Dryden's, but he has seldom elsewhere tried the seven-foot verse as a variation. Strange to say it is far from inharmonious in its place, and has a certain connexion with the sense, though the example certainly cannot be recommended for universal imitation. I cannot remember any instance in another poet of such a licence except the well-known three in the *Revolt of Islam,* which may be thought to be covered by Shelley's prefatory apology.

The direct challenge to the Whigs which the preface contained was not likely to go unanswered; and indeed Dryden had described in it with exact irony the character of the replies he received. Pordage returned to the charge with the *Medal Reversed ;* the admirers of Somers hope that he did not write *Dryden's Satire to his Muse ;* and there were many others. But one of them, the *Medal of John Bayes,* is of considerably greater importance. It was written by Thomas Shadwell, and is perhaps the most scurrilous piece of ribaldry which has ever got itself quoted in English literature. The author gives a life of Dryden, accusing him pell-mell of all sorts of disgraceful conduct and unfortunate experiences. His adulation of Oliver, his puritanic relations, his misfortunes at Cambridge, his marriage, his intrigues with Mrs. Reeve, &c., &c., are all raked up or invented for the purpose of throwing obloquy on him. The attack passed all bounds of decency, especially as it had not been provoked by any personality towards Shadwell, and for once Dryden resolved to make an example of his assailant.

Thomas Shadwell was a Norfolk man and about ten years Dryden's junior. Ever since the year 1668 he had been writing plays (chiefly comedies) and hanging about town, and Dryden and he had been in a manner friends. They had joined Crowne in the task of writing down the *Empress of Morocco*, and it does not appear that Dryden had ever given Shadwell any direct cause of offence. Shadwell, however, who was exceedingly arrogant and apparently jealous of Dryden's acknowledged position as leader of the English drama, took more than one occasion of sneering at Dryden, and especially at his critical prefaces. Not long before the actual declaration of war Shadwell had received a prologue from Dryden, and the outbreak itself was due to purely political causes, though no doubt Shadwell, who was a sincere Whig and Protestant, was very glad to pour out his pent-up literary jealousy at the same time. The personality of his attack on Dryden was, however, in the last degree unwise; for the house in which he lived was of glass almost all over. His manners are admitted to have been coarse and brutal, his conversation unclean, his appearance uninviting; nor was his literary personality safer from attack. He had taken Ben Jonson for his model, and any reader of his comedies must admit that he had a happy knack of detecting or imagining the oddities which, after Ben's example, he called "humours." The *Sullen Lovers* is in this way a much more genuinely amusing play than any of Dryden's, and the *Squire of Alsatia, Bury Fair, Epsom Wells*, the *Virtuoso*, &c., are comedies of manners by no means unimportant for the social history of the time. But whether it was owing to haste, as Rochester pretended, or, as Dryden would have it, to certain intellectual incapacities, there can be no doubt that nobody ever made less use of his faculties than

Shadwell. His work is always disgraceful as writing ; he seems to have been totally destitute of any critical faculty, and he mixes up what is really funny with the dullest and most wearisome folly and ribaldry. He was thus given over entirely into Dryden's hands, and the unmatched satire of *MacFlecknoe* was the result.

Flecknoe, whom but for this work no one would ever have inquired about, was, and had been for some time, a stock-subject for allusive satire. He was an Irish priest who had died not long before, after writing a little good verse and a great deal of bad. He had paid compliments to Dryden, and there is no reason to suppose that Dryden had any enmity towards him ; his part indeed is simply representative, and the satire is reserved for Shadwell. Well as they are known, the first twenty or thirty lines of the poem must be quoted once more, for illustration of Dryden's satirical faculty is hardly possible without them :—

> All human things are subject to decay,
> And, when fate summons, monarchs must obey.
> This Flecknoe found, who, like Augustus, young
> Was called to empire, and had governed long ;
> In prose and verse was owned without dispute,
> Through all the realms of Nonsense, absolute.
> This aged prince, now flourishing in peace,
> And blessed with issue of a large increase,
> Worn out with business, did at length debate
> To settle the succession of the state ;
> And, pondering which of all his sons was fit
> To reign, and wage immortal war with wit,
> Cried—" 'Tis resolved ! for nature pleads, that he
> Should only rule, who most resembles me.
> Shadwell alone my perfect image bears,
> Mature in dulness from his tender years ;
> Shadwell alone, of all my sons, is he
> Who stands confirmed in full stupidity.

> The rest to some faint meaning make pretence,
> But Shadwell never deviates into sense.
> Some beams of wit on other souls may fall,
> Strike through and make a lucid interval;
> But Shadwell's genuine night admits no ray,
> His rising fogs prevail upon the day.
> Besides, his goodly fabric fills the eye,
> And seems designed for thoughtless majesty;
> Thoughtless as monarch oaks, that shade the plain,
> And, spread in solemn state, supinely reign."

MacFlecknoe was published in October, 1682, but Dryden had not done with Shadwell. A month later came out the second part of *Absalom and Achitophel,* in which Nahum Tate took up the story. Tate copied the versification of his master with a good deal of success, though as it is known that Dryden gave strokes almost all through the poem, it is difficult exactly to apportion the other laureate's part. But the second part of *Absalom and Achitophel* would assuredly never be opened were it not for a long passage of about 200 lines, which is entirely Dryden's, and which contains some of his very best work. Unluckily it contains also some of his greatest licences of expression, to which he was probably provoked by the unparalleled language which, as has been said, Shadwell and others had used to him. The 200 lines which he gave Tate are one string of characters, each more savage and more masterly than the last. Ferguson, Forbes, and Johnson are successively branded, Pordage has his ten syllables of immortalizing contempt, and then come the famous characters of Doeg (Settle) and Og (Shadwell),—

> Two fools that crutch their feeble sense on verse,
> Who by my muse to all succeeding times
> Shall live, in spite of their own doggrel rhymes.

The coarseness of speech before alluded to makes it impossible to quote these characters as a whole, but a *cento* is fortunately possible with little loss of vigour.

> Doeg, though without knowing how or why,
> Made still a blundering kind of melody;
> Spurred boldly on, and dashed through thick and thin,
> Through sense and nonsense, never out nor in;
> Free from all meaning, whether good or bad,
> And, in one word, heroically mad,
> He was too warm on picking-work to dwell,
> But fagoted his notions as they fell,
> And, if they rhymed and rattled, all was well.
> Railing in other men may be a crime,
> But ought to pass for mere instinct in him;
> Instinct he follows, and no farther knows,
> For, to write verse with him is to *transprose*;
> 'Twere pity treason at his door to lay,
> Who makes *heaven's gate a lock to its own key;*
> Let him rail on, let his invective muse
> Have four-and-twenty letters to abuse.
> Which, if he jumbles to one line of sense,
> Indict him of a capital offence.
> In fire-works give him leave to vent his spite,
> Those are the only serpents he can write;
> The height of his ambition is, we know,
> But to be master of a puppet-show;
> On that one stage his works may yet appear,
> And a month's harvest keep him all the year.
> Now stop your noses, readers, all and some,
> For here's a tun of midnight work to come,
> Og from a treason-tavern rolling home.
> Round as a globe, and liquored every chink,
> Goodly and great he sails behind his link.
> With all this bulk there's nothing lost in Og,
> For every inch, that is not fool, is rogue.
> The midwife laid her hand on his thick skull,
> With this prophetic blessing—Be thou dull!
> Drink, swear and roar; forbear no lewd delight
> Fit for thy bulk, do anything but write.
> Thou art of lasting make, like thoughtless men,
> A strong nativity—but for the pen;

Eat opium, mingle arsenic in thy drink,
Still thou mayest live, avoiding pen and ink.
I see, I see, 'tis counsel given in vain,
For treason, botched in rhyme, will be thy bane ;
Rhyme is the rock on which thou art to wreck,
'Tis fatal to thy fame and to thy neck.
Why should thy metre good king David blast ?
A psalm of his will surely be thy last.
A double noose thou on thy neck dost pull
For writing treason, and for writing dull ;
To die for faction is a common evil,
But to be hanged for nonsense is the devil.
Hadst thou the glories of thy king exprest,
Thy praises had been satire at the best ;
But thou in clumsy verse, unlickt, unpointed,
Hast shamefully defied the Lord's anointed :
I will not rake the dunghill of thy crimes,
For who would read thy life that reads thy rhymes ?
But of king David's foes, be this the doom,
May all be like the young man Absalom ;
And for my foes may this their blessing be,
To talk like Doeg, and to write like thee.

No one, I think, can fail to recognize here the qualities
which have already been set forth as specially distinguishing Dryden's satire, the fund of truth at the bottom of it,
the skilful adjustment of the satire so as to make faults of
the merits which are allowed, the magnificent force and
variety of the verse, and the constant maintenance of a
kind of superior contempt never degenerating into mere
railing or losing its superiority in petty spite. The last
four verses in especial might almost be taken as a model
of satirical verse.

These verses were the last that Dryden wrote in the
directly satirical way. His four great poems—the two
parts of *Absalom and Achitophel*, the *Medal*, and *Mac-
Flecknoe*, had been produced in rather more than a year,
and, high as was his literary position before, had exalted

him infinitely higher. From this time forward there
could be no doubt at all of his position, with no second at
any moderate distance, at the head of living Englishmen of
letters. He was now to earn a new title to this position.
Almost simultaneously with the second part of *Absalom
and Achitophel* appeared *Religio Laici*.

Scott has described *Religio Laici* as one of the most
admirable poems in the language, which in some respects
it undoubtedly is; but it is also one of the most singular.
That a man who had never previously displayed any particular interest in theological questions, and who had
reached the age of fifty-one, with a reputation derived,
until quite recently, in the main from the composition of
loose plays, should appear before his public of pleasure-
seekers with a serious argument in verse on the credibility
of the Christian religion and the merits of the Anglican
form of doctrine and church government would nowadays
be something more than a nine days' wonder. In Dryden's
time it was somewhat less surprising. The spirit of
theological controversy was bred in the bone of the seventeenth century. It will always remain an instance of the
subordination in Macaulay of the judicial to the advo-
cating faculty, that he who knew the time so well should
have adduced the looseness of Dryden's plays as an argument against the sincerity of his conversion. It is quite
certain that James the Second was both a man of loose life
and of thoroughly sincere religious belief; it is by no means
certain that his still more profligate brother's unbelief was
not a mere assumption, and generally it may be noted
that the biographies of the time never seem to infer any
connexion between irregularity of life and unsoundness
of religious faith. I have already shown some cause for
disbelieving the stories, or rather the assertions, of Dryden's

profligacy, though even these would not be conclusive
against his sincerity ; but I believe that it would be
difficult to trace any very active concern in him for
things religious before the Popish Plot. Various circumstances already noticed may then have turned his mind
to the subject, and that active and vigorous mind when it
once attacked a subject rarely deserted it. Consistency
was in no matter Dryden's great characteristic, and the
arguments of *Religio Laici* are not more inconsistent
with the arguments of *The Hind and the Panther* than
the handling of the question of rhymed plays in the
Essay of dramatic poesy is with the arguments against
them in the prefaces and dissertations subsequent to
Aurengzebe.

It has sometimes been sought to give *Religio Laici* a
political as well as a religious sense, and to connect it in
this way with the series of political satires, with the
Duke of Guise and with the subsequent *Hind and Panther.*
The connexion, however, seems to me to be faint. The
struggles of the Popish Plot had led to the contests on
the Exclusion Bill on the one hand, and they had re-
opened the controversial question between the Churches
of England and Rome on the other. They had thus in
different ways given rise to *Absalom and Achitophel* and
to *Religio Laici*, but the two poems have no community
but a community of origin. Indeed, the suspicion of
any political design in *Religio Laici* is not only groundless but contradictory. The views of James on the subject were known to every one, and those of Charles
himself are not likely to have been wholly hidden from
an assiduous follower of the court, and a friend of the
king's greatest intimates, like Dryden. Still less is it
necessary to take account of the absurd suggestion that

Dryden wrote the poem as a stepping-stone to orders and to ecclesiastical preferment. He has definitely denied that he had at any time thoughts of entering the church, and such thoughts are certainly not likely to have occurred to him at the age of fifty. The poem therefore, as it seems to me, must be regarded as a genuine production, expressing the author's first thoughts on a subject which had just presented itself to him as interesting and important. Such first thoughts in a mind like Dryden's, which was by no means a revolutionary mind, and which was disposed to accept the church as part and parcel of the Tory system of principles, were pretty certain to take the form of an apologetic harmonizing of difficulties and doubts. The author must have been familiar with the usual objections of the persons vaguely called Hobbists, and with the counter-objections of the Romanists. He takes them both and he makes the best of them.

In its form and arrangement *Religio Laici* certainly deserves the praise which critics have given it. Dryden's overtures are very generally among the happiest parts of his poems, and the opening ten or twelve lines of this poem are among his very best. The bold *enjambement* of the first two couplets, with the striking novelty of cadence given by the sharply cut *cæsura* of the third line, is one of his best metrical effects, and the actual picture of the cloudy night-sky and the wandering traveller matches the technical beauty of the verse. The rest of the poem is studiously bare of ornament, and almost exclusively argumentative. There is and could be nothing specially novel or extraordinarily forcible in the arguments; but they are put with that ease and apparent cogency which have been already remarked upon as characterizing all Dryden's didactic work. The poem is not without

touches of humour, and winds up with a characteristic
but not ill-humoured fling at the unhappy Shadwell.

Dryden's next productions of importance were two odes
of the so-called Pindaric kind. The example of Cowley
had made this style very popular; but Dryden himself
had not practised it. The years 1685-6 gave him occasion to do so. His *Threnodia Augustalis* or funeral
poem on Charles the Second may be taken as the chief
official production of his laureateship. The difficulties of
such performances are well known, and the reproaches
brought against their faults are pretty well stereotyped.
Threnodia Augustalis is not exempt from the faults of its
kind; but it has merits which for that kind are decidedly
unusual. The stanza which so adroitly at once praises
and satirizes Charles's patronage of literary men is perhaps
the best, and certainly the best known; but the termination is also fine. Of very different merit, however, is
the *Ode to the Memory of Mrs. Anne Killegrew*. This
elegy is among the best of many noble funeral poems
which Dryden wrote. The few lines on the Marquis
of Winchester, the incomparable address to Oldham—
" Farewell, too little and too lately known "—and at a
later date the translated epitaph on Claverhouse are all
remarkable; but the Killegrew elegy is of far greater importance. It is curious that in these days of selections no
one has attempted a collection of the best regular and
irregular odes in English. There are not many of them,
but a small anthology could be made reaching from Milton
to Mr. Swinburne, which would contain some remarkable
poetry. Among these the ode to Anne Killegrew would
assuredly hold a high place. Johnson pronounced it the
noblest in the language, and in his time it certainly was,
unless *Lycidas* be called an ode. Since its time there

has been Wordsworth's great immortality ode, and certain beautiful but fragmentary pieces of Shelley which might be so classed ; but till our own days nothing else which can match this. The first stanza may be pronounced absolutely faultless and incapable of improvement. As a piece of concerted music in verse it has not a superior, and Warton's depreciation of it is a curious instance of the lack of catholic taste which has so often marred English criticism of poetry :—

> Thou youngest virgin-daughter of the skies,
>   Made in the last promotion of the blessed ;
> Whose palms, new plucked from Paradise,
> In spreading branches more sublimely rise,
>   Rich with immortal green above the rest :
> Whether, adopted to some neighbouring star,
> Thou rollest above us, in thy wandering race,
>   Or, in procession fixed and regular,
>   Movest with the heaven's majestic pace ;
>   Or, called to more superior bliss,
> Thou treadest with seraphims the vast abyss :
> Whatever happy region is thy place,
> Cease thy celestial song a little space;
> Thou wilt have time enough for hymns divine,
>   Since Heaven's eternal year is thine.
> Hear, then, a mortal Muse thy praise rehearse,
>   In no ignoble verse ;
> But such as thy own voice did practise here,
> When thy first fruits of Poesy were given,
> To make thyself a welcome inmate there ;
>   While yet a young probationer,
>   And candidate of heaven.

These smaller pieces were followed at some interval by the remarkable poem which is Dryden's chief work, if bulk and originality of plan are taken into consideration. There is a tradition as to the place of composition of *The Hind and the Panther*, which in many respects deserves

to be true, though there is apparently no direct testimony
to its truth. It is said to have been written at Rushton
not far from Kettering, in the poet's native county.
Rushton had been (though it had passed from them at
this time) the seat of the Treshams, one of the staunchest
families to the old faith which Dryden had just embraced.
They had held another seat in Northamptonshire—Lyveden, within a few miles of Aldwinkle and of all the
scenes of the poet's youth; and both at Lyveden and
Rushton, architectural evidences of their devotion to the
cause survive in the shape of buildings covered with
symbolical carvings. The neighbourhood of Rushton,
too, is singularly consonant to the scenery of the poem.
It lay just on the southern fringe of the great forest of
Rockingham, and the neighbourhood is still wonderfully
timbered, though most of the actual wood owes its existence to the planting energy of Duke John of Montagu,
half a century after Dryden's time. It would certainly
not have been easy to conceive a better place for the conception and execution of this sylvan poem; but, as a
matter of fact, it seems impossible to obtain any definite
evidence of the connexion between the two.

The Hind and the Panther is in plan a sort of combina-
tion of *Absalom and Achitophel*, and of *Religio Laici*,
but its three parts are by no means homogeneous. The
first part, which is perhaps on the whole the best, contains the well-known apportionment of the characters of
different beasts to the different churches and sects; the
second contains the major part of the controversy between
the Hind and the Panther; the third, which is as long
as the other two put together, continues this controversy,
but before very long diverges into allegorical and personal
satire. The story of the Swallows, which the Panther

tells, is one of the liveliest of all Dryden's pieces of narration, and it is not easy to give the palm between it and the Hind's retort, the famous fable of the Doves, in which Burnet is caricatured with hardly less vigour and not much less truth than Buckingham and Shadwell in the satires proper. This told, the poem ends abruptly.

The Hind and the Panther was certain to provoke controversy, especially from the circumstances, presently to be discussed, under which it was written. Dryden had two points especially vulnerable, the one being personal the other literary. It was inevitable that his argument in *Religio Laici* should be contrasted with his argument in *The Hind and the Panther*. It was inevitable on the other hand that the singularities of construction in the latter poem should meet with animadversion. No defender of *The Hind and the Panther*, indeed, has ever attempted to defend it as a regular or classically proportioned piece of work. Its main theme is, as always with Dryden, merely a canvas whereon to embroider all sorts of episodes, digressions and ornaments. Yet his adversaries, in their blind animosity, went a great deal too far in the matter of condemnation, and showed themselves entirely ignorant of the history and requirements of allegory in general, and the beast-fable in particular. Dryden, like many other great men of letters, had an admiration for the incomparable story of Reynard the fox. It is characteristic, both of his enemies and of the age, that this was made a serious argument against him. This is specially done in a celebrated little pamphlet which has perhaps had the honour of being more overpraised than anything else of its kind in English literature. If any one wishes to appraise the value of the story that Dryden was seriously vexed by *The Hind and the Panther trans-*

H

versed to the Story of the City and Country Mouse, he
cannot do better than read that production. It is difficult to say what was or was not unworthy of Montague,
whose published poems certainly do not authorize us to
say that he wrote below himself on this occasion, but it
assuredly is in the highest degree unworthy of Prior.
Some tolerable parody of Dryden's own work, a good
deal of heavy joking closely modelled on the *Rehearsal* and
assigning to Mr. Bayes plenty of "i'gads" and the like
catchwords, make up the staple of this piece, in which
Mr. Christie has discovered "true wit," and the Quarterly
Reviewer already cited, "exquisite satire." Among the
severest of Messrs. Montague and Prior's strictures is a
sarcastic reference to Reynard the fox. What was good
enough for Dryden, for Goethe, and for Mr. Carlyle was
childish rubbish to these brisk young critics. The story
alluded to says that Dryden wept at the attack and com-
plained that two young fellows to whom he had been civil
should thus have treated an old man. Now Dryden
certainly did not consider himself an old man at this
time, and he had "seen many others," as an admirable
Gallicism has it, in the matter of attacks.

One more poem, and one only, remains to be noticed in
this division. This was the luckless *Britannia Rediviva,*
written on the birth of the most ill-starred of all Princes
of Wales, born in the purple. It is in couplets, and as
no work of Dryden's written at this time could be
worthless, it contains some vigorous verse, but on the
whole it is by far the worst of his serious poems ; and it
was no misfortune for his fame that the Revolution left it
out of print for the rest of the author's life.

CHAPTER V.

THAT portion of Dryden's life which extends from the
Popish Plot to the Revolution is of so much more importance for the estimate of his personal character, as well
as for that of his literary genius, than any other period
of equal length, that it has seemed well to devote a
separate chapter to the account and discussion of it.
The question of Dryden's conversion, its motives and its
sincerity, has of itself been more discussed than any other
point in his life, and on the opinions to be formed of it
must depend the opinion which, on the whole, we form of
him as a man. According to one view his conduct during
these years places him among the class which paradox
delights to describe as the "greatest and meanest of mankind," the men who compensate for the admirable qualities
of their heads by the despicable infirmities of their hearts.
According to another, his conduct, if not altogether wise,
contains nothing discreditable to him, and some things
which may be reasonably described as very much the
contrary. Twenty years of play-writing had, in all probability, somewhat disgusted Dryden with the stage, and
his Rose-Alley misfortune had shown him that even a
scrupulous abstinence from meddling in politics or in personal satire would not save him from awkward conse-

quences. His lucrative contract with the players had,
beyond all doubt, ceased, and his official salaries, as we
shall see, were paid with the usual irregularity. At the
same time, as has been already pointed out, his turn
of thought probably led him to take more interest in
practical politics and in religious controversy than had
been previously the case. The additional pension,
which as we have seen he had received, made his
nominal income sufficient, and instead of writing plays
invitâ Minervâ he took to writing satires and argumentative pieces to please himself. Other crumbs of royal
favour fell to his lot from time to time. The broad pieces
received for the *Medal* are very probably apocryphal, but
there is no doubt that his youngest son received, in
February, 1683, a presentation to the Charterhouse from
the king. This presentation it was which he was said to have
received from Shaftesbury, as the price of the mitigating
lines ("Yet fame deserved—easy of access") inserted in the
later edition of *Absalom and Achitophel*. He was also
indefatigable in undertaking and performing minor literary
work of various kinds, which will be noticed later. Nor
indeed could he afford to be idle ; his pensions were often
unpaid, and it is just after the great series of his satires
closed that we get a glimpse of this fact. A letter is extant to Rochester—Hyde, not Wilmot—complaining of long
arrears, and entreating some compensation in the shape of
a place in the Customs, or the Excise, besides an instal-
ment at least of the debt. It is this letter which contains
the well-known phrase, " It is enough for one age to have
neglected Mr. Cowley and starved Mr. Butler." As far
as documentary evidence goes the answer to the appeal
was a Treasury warrant for 75*l.*, the arrears being over
1000*l.*, and an appointment to a collectorship of Customs

in the port of London, with unknown emoluments. The
only definite sum mentioned is a nominal one of 5*l.* a
year as collector of duties on cloth. But it is not likely
that cloth was the only subject of Dryden's labours,
and in those days the system of fees and perquisites
flourished. This Customs appointment was given in
1683.

To the condition of Dryden's sentiments in the last
years of Charles' reign *Religio Laici* must be taken as the
surest, and indeed as the only clue. There is no proof
that this poem was composed to serve any political purpose, and indeed it could not have served any, neither
James nor Charles being likely to be propitiated by a defence, however moderate and rationalizing, of the Church
of England. It is not dedicated to any patron, and seems
to have been an altogether spontaneous expression of what
was passing in the poet's mind. A careful study of the
poem, instead of furnishing arguments against the sincerity of his subsequent conduct, furnishes, I think, on
the contrary, arguments which are very strongly in its
favour. It could have, as has just been said, no purpose
of pleasing a lay patron, for there was none to be pleased
by it. It is not at all likely to have commended itself to
a clerical patron, because of its rationalizing tone, its
halting adoption of the Anglican Church as a kind of make-
shift, and its heterodox yearnings after infallibility. These
last indeed are among the most strongly-marked features
of the piece, and point most clearly in the direction which
the poet afterwards took.

> Such an omniscient church we wish indeed,
> 'Twere worth both Testaments, cast in the Creed,

is an awkward phrase for a sound divine, or a dutifully

acquiescing layman; but it is exactly the phrase which
might be expected from a man who was on the slope from
placid caring for none of these things to a more or less
fervent condition of membership of an infallible church.
The tenor of the whole poem, as it seems to me, is the
same. The author, in his character of high Tory and
orthodox Englishman, endeavours to stop himself at the
point which the Anglican Church marks with a thus far
and no farther; but, in a phrase which has no exact
English equivalent, *nous le voyons venir*. It is quite
evident that if he continues to feel anything like a lively
interest in the problems at stake, he will go further still.
He did go further, and has been accordingly railed against
for many generations. But I do not hesitate to put the
question to the present generation in a very concrete form.
Is Dryden's critic nowadays prepared to question the
sincerity of Cardinal Newman? If he is I have no
objection to his questioning the sincerity of Dryden. But
what is sauce for the nineteenth-century goose is surely
sauce for the seventeenth-century gander. The post-con-
version writings of the Cardinal are not less superficially
inconsistent with the *Tracts for the Times* and the *Oxford
Sermons*, than the *Hind and the Panther* is with *Religio
Laici*.

A hyperbole has been in some sort necessary in order to
rebut the very unjust aspersions which two of the most
popular historians of the last thirty years have thrown on
Dryden. But I need hardly say, that though the glory of
Oxford in the first half of the nineteenth century is a fair
argumentative parallel to the glory of Cambridge in the
second half of the seventeenth, the comparison is not intended to be forced. I believe Dryden to have been, in the
transactions of the years 1685-7, thoroughly sincere as far as

conscious sincerity went, but of a certain amount of un-
conscious insincerity I am by no means disposed to acquit
him. If I judge his character aright, no English man of
letters was ever more thoroughly susceptible to the spirit
and influence of his time. Dryden was essentially a
literary man, and was disposed rather to throw himself
into the arms of any party than into those of one so hopelessly unliterary as the ultra-Liberal and ultra-Protestant
party of the seventeenth century was. He was moreover
a professed servant of the public, or as we should put it
in these days, he had the journalist spirit. Fortunately—
and it is for everybody who has to do with literature the
most fortunate sign of the times—it is not now necessary
for any one to do violence to a single opinion, even to a
single crotchet of his own, in order to make his living by
his pen. It was not so in Dryden's days, and it is fully
believable that a sense that he was about to be on the
winning side may have assisted his rapid determination
from Hobbism or Halifaxism to Romanist orthodoxy. I
am the more disposed to this allowance because it seems
to me that Dryden's principal decrier was in need of a
similar charity. Lord Macaulay is at present a glory of
the Whigs. If there had been an equal opening when he
was a young man for distinction and profit as a Tory,
for early retirement on literary pursuits with a compe-
tence, and for all the other things which he most desired,
is it quite so certain that he would not have been of the
other persuasion ? I have heard persons much more
qualified than I am to decide on the characteristics of
pure Liberalism energetically repudiate Macaulay's claim
to be an apostle thereof. Yet I for my part have not the
least idea of challenging his sincerity. It seems to me
that he would have been at least wise if he had refrained,

considering the insufficiency of his knowledge, from challenging the sincerity of Dryden.

How insufficient the knowledge was the labours of subsequent investigators have sufficiently shown. Mr. Bell proved that the pension supposed to be conferred by James as a reward for Dryden's apostasy was simply a renewal of the pension granted by Charles years before; that it preceded instead of following the conversion, and that the sole reason of its having to be renewed at all was technical merely. As for the argument about Dryden's being previously indifferent to religion, and having written indecent plays, the arguer has himself demolished his argument in a famous passage about James's own morals, and the conduct of the non-resistance doctors of the Anglican Church. Burnet's exaggerated denunciations of Dryden as a "monster of impurity of all sorts," &c., are sufficiently traceable to Shadwell's shameless libels and to the Character of the Buzzard. It is true that the allegations of Malone and Scott, to the effect that Lady Elizabeth had been already converted, and Charles Dryden likewise, rest on a very slender foundation; but these are matters which have very little to do with the question in any case. The real problem can be very easily stated. Given a man to the general rectitude of whose private conduct all qualified witnesses testify, while it is only questioned by unscrupulous libellers—who gained, as can be proved, not one penny by his conversion, and though he subsequently lost heavily by it maintained it unswervingly—who can be shown, from the most unbiassed of his previous writings, to have been in exactly the state of mind which was likely to result in such a proceeding, and of whose insincerity there is no proof of the smallest value—what reason is there for suspecting him? The literary greatness of the man has nothing to do with the question. The fact is that he has been convicted, or rather sentenced, on evidence which would not suffice to convict Elkanah Settle or Samuel Pordage.

In particular we have a right to insist upon the absolute consistency of Dryden's subsequent conduct. Mr. Christie, who, admirably as for the most part he judges Dryden's literary work, was steeled against his personal character by the fact that Dryden attacked his idol Shaftesbury, thinks that a recantation would have done him no good had he tried it. The opinion is, to say the least, hasty. Had Dryden proffered the oaths to William and Mary, as poet-laureate and historiographer, it is very hard to see what power could have deprived him of his two hundred a year. The extra hundred of pension might have been forfeited, but the revenues of these places, and of that in the Customs must have been safe, unless the new Government chose to incur what it was of all things desirous to prevent, the charge of persecution and intolerance. When the Whigs were so desperately hard up for literary talent that Dorset, in presenting Shadwell for the laureateship, had to pay him the very left-handed compliment of saying, that if he was not the best poet he was at least the honestest—i. e. the most orthodoxly Whiggish—man, when hardly a single distinguished man of letters save Locke, who was nothing of a pamphleteer, was on their side, is it to be supposed for a moment that Dryden would not have been welcome? The argument against him recalls a curious and honourable story which Johnson tells of Smith, the Bohemian author of *Phædra and Hippolytus*. Addison, who, as all the world knows, was a friend of Smith's, and who was always ready to do his friends good turns, procured for Smith, from some Whig

magnates, a commission for a History of the Revolution.
To the disgust of the mediator Smith demurred. "What,"
he said, " am I to do with the character of Lord Sunderland ?" Addison is said to have replied, in deep but
illogical wrath, "When were you drunk last?" I feel
extremely inclined to put Smith's query to the persons
who maintain that it would have been impossible for
Dryden to turn his coat at the Revolution. What are
they going to do with the character of Lord Sunderland?
In the age not merely of Sunderland, but of Marlborough,
of Godolphin, of Russell, of a hundred other treble-dyed
traitors, it surely cannot be contended that the first living
writer of English would have been rejected by those who
had need of his services. Now, we know that so far from
making any overtures of submission, Dryden was stiff in
his Jacobitism and in his faith. Nothing in his life is
more celebrated than his persistent refusal to give way
to Tonson's entreaties to dedicate the Virgil to William,
and his whole post-Revolution works may be searched in
vain for a single stroke intended to curry favour with the
powers that were. If, as he puts it in a letter still extant,
they would take him on his literary merits, he would not
refuse their offers, but as to yielding an inch of his principles, he would not. And his works amply justify the
brave words. It is surely hard measure to go out of one's
way to upbraid with wanton or venal apostasy one to
whose sincerity there is such complete testimony, both *a
priori* and *a posteriori*, as this.

Except the *Hind and the Panther* no work inspired by
his new religious sentiments did Dryden much credit, or, it
would appear, brought him much profit. James was not
a particularly generous master, though it is probable that
the laureate-historiographer-collector received his dues

much more punctually under his orderly administration
than in the days of his spendthrift brother. The works
upon which the court put Dryden were not very happily
chosen, nor in all cases very happily executed. His defence
of the reasons which had converted Anne Hyde, is about
the worst of his prose works, and was handled (in the
rough controversial fashion of the day) very damagingly
by Stillingfleet. A translation of a work of Varillas' on
ecclesiastical history was announced but never published,
and considering the worthlessness of Varillas as a historian
it is just as well. The *Life of St. Francis Xavier*, dedicated to the queen, was better worth doing, and was well
done. It is curious that in this dedication occurs one of
those confident anticipations of the birth of the young
Pretender, which after the event were used by zealous
Protestants as arguments for the spuriousness of the child.
These and minor works show that Dryden, as indeed might
be expected, was in favour at court, and was made use of
by the economical and pious rulers of England. But of
any particular benefit reaped by him from his conversion
there is no hint whatever ; in some respects, indeed, it did
him harm. His two youngest sons, who had followed
their father's change of faith, were elected about this
time to scholarships at the universities, but were prevented, apparently by their religion, from going into
residence.

The mere loss of education and prospects for his children
was, however, a trifle to what Dryden had to undergo at
the Revolution. It is probable that this event was almost
as much a surprise to him as to James himself. But however severe the blow might be it was steadily borne. The
period at which the oaths had to be taken to the new
Government came, and Dryden did not take them. This

vacated at once his literary posts and his place in the Customs, if, as there seems every reason to believe, he held it up to the time. His position was now exceedingly serious. He was nearly sixty years of age. His patrimony was but small, and such addition to it as he had received with Lady Elizabeth did not exceed a few scores of pounds annually. He had three sons grown to man's estate, and all the more difficult to provide for that their religion incapacitated them from almost every profitable pursuit in their native country. He himself had long, save in one trifling instance, broken his relation with the stage, the most lucrative opening for literary work. He was a marked man, far more obnoxious personally to many of the ruling party than Milton had been thirty years before, when he thought it necessary to go into "abscondence." The very gains of the theatre were not what they had been, unless they were enhanced by assiduous visits to patrons and dedicatees, a degrading performance to which Dryden never would consent. Loss of fortune, of prospects, and of powerful friends was accompanied in Dryden's case by the most galling annoyances to his self-love. His successor in the laureateship was none other than Shadwell, whom he had so bitterly satirized, whom he had justly enough declared able to do anything but write, and who was certain to exult over him with all the triumph of a coarse and vindictive nature. Dryden, however, came out of the trial admirably. He had indeed some staunch friends in both political parties, the Dorsets and the Leveson-Gowers being as true to him as the Rochesters and the Ormonds. But his main resource now, as all through his life, was his incomparable literary faculty, his splendid capacity for work, and his dogged opposition to the assaults of fortune. In the twelve years of life

which remained to him he built up his fortune and
maintained it anew, not merely by assiduous practice of
those forms of literature in which he had already won
renown, but by exercising yet again his marvellous talent
for guessing the taste of the time, and striking out new
lines to please it. Just as no one from *Annus Mirabilis* and
Aurengzebe could have divined *Absalom and Achitophel*
and the *Hind and the Panther*, so no one, except on the
principle that all things were now possible to Dryden, could
have divined from *Absalom and Achitophel* and the *Hind
and the Panther*, either *Palamon and Arcite*, or the translation of Virgil.

Some minor works of Dryden's not mentioned in the
last chapter, nor falling under the heads to be noticed in
subsequent chapters, may here deserve notice. Some time
or other in the reign of James the Second Dryden wrote
to Etherege a poetical epistle, which is its author's only
attempt in the easy octosyllabic verse, which Butler had
just used with such brilliant success, and which Prior was
in a more polished if less vigorous form to use with success almost equally brilliant a few years later. " Gentle
George " Etherege deserved the compliments which Dryden
paid him more than once, and it is only to be wished that
the poet's communications with him, whether in verse or
prose, had been more frequent. Had they been so we
might have been able to solve what is now one of the most
curious problems of English literary history. Though Etherege was a man of fashion, of literary importance, and of
a distinguished position in diplomacy—he was English
minister at Ratisbon, where Dryden addresses him—only
the circumstances and not the date of his death are known.
It is said that in seeing his friends downstairs he over-
balanced himself and was taken up dead ; but when this

happened no one seems to know.[1] A line in the epistle seems to show that Etherege had been obliged to take to heavy drinking as a compliment to his German friends, and thus indirectly prophesies the circumstances of his death. But the author of *Sir Fopling Flutter* and *She would if she could* hardly deserved such a hugger-mugger end.

To this time too belongs the first *Ode on St. Cecilia's Day*. It is not a great production, and cannot pretend comparison with the second and more famous piece composed on a later occasion. But it is curious how many lines and phrases it has contributed to the list of stock quotations—especially curious when it is remembered that the whole piece is only sixty-three lines long. " A heap of jarring atoms," " the diapason closing full in man," " the double, double, double beat of the thundering drum," and several other phrases survive. The thing was set to music by an Italian composer named Draghi, and seems to have been popular. Besides these and other tasks Dryden began at this time a curious work or series of works, which was continued at intervals till his death, which was imitated afterwards by many others, and which in some sort was an ancestor of the modern literary magazine or review. This was the *Miscellany*, the first volume of which appeared in the beginning of 1684, and the second

[1] In reply to a request of mine, Mr. W. Noel Sainsbury has brought to my notice letters of Etherege in the Record Office and in the Reports of the Historical MSS. Commission. In January, 1688-9, Etherege wrote to Lord Preston from Ratisbon. The first letter from his successor is dated April, 1689. If then he died at Ratisbon this brings the date between narrow limits. There is, however, a rival legend that he followed James into exile. Since this note was written more letters have, I hear, been found in the British Museum, and Mr. Gosse has the whole subject under treatment.

in the beginning of 1685, though a considerable interval occurred before a third volume was brought out. These volumes contained both old and new poems, mostly of the occasional kind, by Dryden himself, besides many of his translations. But they were by no means limited to his own productions. Many other authors, old and new, were admitted, and to the second volume Charles Dryden, his eldest son, was a contributor. These two years (1684 and 1685), it will be observed, were not merely those in which, owing to the non-payment of his appointments, his pecuniary straits must have been considerable, but they were also years in which there was a kind of lull between the rapid series of his great satirical works and the collection of verse and prose productions which owe their birth to his conversion. It is somewhat remarkable that Dryden's abstinence from the stage during this time —which was broken only by the *Duke of Guise* and by the production of the rather unsuccessful opera, *Albion and Albanius*—seems to have been accompanied by a cessation also in his activity as a prologue writer. Both before and after this period prologue writing was a regular source of income and employment to him. There is a famous story of Southerne and Dryden which is often quoted, both for its intrinsic interest, and because the variety with which its circumstances are related is rather an instructive comment on the trustworthiness of such stories. Every one is supposed to know Pope's reference to the author of *Oroonoko* as—

> Tom whom heaven sent down to raise
> The price of prologues and of plays.

The story is that Southerne in 1782 applied to Dryden for a prologue (which is extant), and was told that the

tariff had gone up from two guineas to three. "Not out
of any disrespect to you, young man, but the players have
had my goods too cheap." The figur..s two and three are
replaced in some versions by four and six, in others by
five and ten. This story gives the date of 1682, and it is
remarkable that until 1690, when Dryden once more came
on the stage himself with a new play, his prologues and
epilogues are very few. Possibly the increased price was
prohibitive, but it is more likely that the political struggles
of the time put all but political verse out of fashion.
These compositions had always been famous, or rather in-
famous, for their licence of language, and the political
excesses of some of Dryden's few utterances of the kind at
this time are not creditable to his memory. Hallam's phrase
of "virulent ribaldry" is absurd as applied to *Absalom
and Achitophel*, or to the *Medal*. It is only too well in
place as applied to the stuff put in the mouth of the
actress who spoke the epilogue to the *Duke of Guise*.
The truth is that if they be taken as a whole these prologues and epilogues could be better spared by lovers of
Dryden from his works than any other section thereof;
and it is particularly to be regretted that Mr. Christie, in
his excellent Globe edition of the poems, has admitted
them, while excluding the always melodious, and sometimes exquisitely poetical songs from the plays, which certainly do not exceed the prologues in licence of language,
while their literary merit is incomparably greater.

CHAPTER VI.

IT might have seemed, at first sight, that the Revolution would be a fatal blow to Dryden. Being unwilling to take the oaths to the new Government, he lost at once the places and the pensions which, irregularly as they had been paid, had made up, since he ceased to write constantly for the stage, by far the greater part of his income. He was nearly sixty years old, his private fortune was, if not altogether insignificant, quite insufficient for his wants, and he had three sons to maintain and set out in the world. But he faced the ruin of his fortunes, and what must have been bitterer to him, the promotion of his enemies into his own place, with the steady courage and practical spirit of resource which were among his most creditable characteristics. Not all his friends deserted him, and from Dorset in particular he received great and apparently constant assistance. The story that this generous patron actually compensated Dryden by an annuity equal in value to his former appointments seems to rest on insufficient foundation. The story that when Dryden and Tom Brown dined with Dorset the one found a hundred-pound note and the other a fifty-pound note under his cover, does not do much credit to Dorset's powers of literary arithmetic,

I

nor, even allowing for the simpler manners of the time, to
his delicacy of feeling. But Dryden's own words are
explicit on the point of his having received assistance from
this old friend, and it is said that in certain letters preserved at Knole, and not yet given to the world, there
are still more definite acknowledgments. Dryden, however, was never disposed to depend on patrons, even
though, like Corneille, he did not think it necessary
to refuse their gifts when they presented themselves.
Theatrical gains had, it has been said, decreased, unless
dramatists took pains to increase them by dedication or by
the growing practice of placing subscription copies among
wealthy friends. Still, a hundred pounds could be depended upon from a good third night and from the bookseller's fee for the book, and a hundred pounds was a
matter of considerable importance to Dryden just now.
For full seven years he had all but abandoned dramatic
composition. His contributions to Lee's *Duke of Guise*,
which probably brought him no money, and certainly
brought him a troublesome controversy, and the opera of
Albion and Albanius had been his only attempts on the
stage since the *Spanish Friar*. The *Duke of Guise*, though
Dryden's part in it is of no little merit, hardly needs
notice here, and *Albion and Albanius* was a failure. It
was rather a masque than an opera, and depended, though
there is some good verse in it, rather on elaborate and
spiteful gibbeting of the enemies of the court than on
poetical or dramatic merits. But Dryden's dramatic reputation was by no means impaired. The first play ordered
to be performed by Queen Mary was the *Spanish Friar*,
and this Protestant drama proved a most unfortunate one
for her Majesty; for the audience at that time were
extraordinarily quick to seize any kind of political allusion,

and, as it happened, there were in the *Spanish Friar*
many allusions of an accidental but unmistakable kind to
ungrateful children, banished monarchs, and so forth. The
eyes of the whole audience were fixed on Mary, and she
probably repented of her choice. But Dryden did not
long depend on revivals of his old plays. The second
year of the new régime saw the production of *Don
Sebastian*, a tragi-comedy, one scene of which, that
between Sebastian and Dorax, is famous in literature,
and which as a whole is often ranked above all Dryden's
other dramas, though for my own part I prefer *All for
Love*. The play, though at first received with a certain
lukewarmness, which may have been due to various causes,
soon became very popular. It was dedicated to Lord
Leicester, Algernon Sidney's eldest brother, a very old
man, who was probably almost alone among his contemporaries (with the exception of Dryden himself) in being an
ardent admirer of Chaucer. In the preface to the *Fables*
the poet tells us that he had postponed his translation
of the elder bard out of deference to Lord Leicester's
strongly expressed opinion that the text should be left
alone. In the same year was produced a play less original,
but perhaps almost better, and certainly more popular.
This was *Amphitryon*, which some critics have treated
most mistakenly as a mere translation of Molière. The
truth is that the three plays of Plautus, Molière, and
Dryden are remarkable examples of the power which
great writers have of treading in each other's steps without servile imitation. In a certain dry humour Dryden's
play is inferior to Plautus, but, as compared with Molière,
it has two features which are decided improvements—the
introduction of the character of Judge Gripus and the
separation of the part of the Soubrette into two. As *Don*

Sebastian had been dedicated to Lord Leicester, an old Cromwellian, so *Amphitryon* was dedicated to Sir William Leveson Gower, a prominent Williamite. Neither dedication contains the least truckling to the powers that were, but Dryden seems to have taken a pleasure in showing that men of both parties were sensible of his merit and of the hardship of his position. Besides these two plays an alteration of *The Prophetess* was produced in 1690, in which Dryden is said to have assisted Betterton. In 1691 appeared *King Arthur*, a masque-opera on the plan of *Albion and Albanius*. Unlike the latter, it has no political meaning; indeed, Dryden confesses to having made considerable alterations in it, in order to make it non-political. The former piece had been set by a Frenchman, Grabut, and the music had been little thought of. Purcell undertook the music for *King Arthur* with much better success. Allowing for a certain absurdity which always besets the musical drama, and which is particularly apparent in that of the late seventeenth and early eighteenth century, *King Arthur* is a very good piece ; the character of Emmeline is attractive, the supernatural part is managed with a skill which would have been almost proof against the wits of the *Rehearsal*, and many of the lyrics are excellent. Dryden was less fortunate with his two remaining dramas. In writing the first he showed himself, for so old a craftsman and courtier, very unskilful in the choice of a subject. *Cleomenes*, the banished King of Sparta, could not but awaken the susceptibilities of zealous revolution censors. After some difficulties, in which Laurence Hyde once more did Dryden a good turn, the piece was licensed, but it was not very successful. It contains some fine passages, but the most remarkable thing about it is that there is a considerable relapse into rhyme, which Dryden

had abandoned for many years. It contains, also, one of
the last, not the least beautiful, and fortunately almost
the most quotable of the exquisite lyrics which, while
they prove perhaps more fully than anything else, Dryden's
almost unrivalled command of versification, disprove at
the same time his alleged incapacity to express true
feeling.   Here it is :—

> No, no, poor suffering heart, no change endeavour,
> Choose to sustain the smart, rather than leave her ;
> My ravished eyes behold such charms about her,
> I can die with her, but not live without her ;
> One tender sigh of hers to see me languish,
> Will more than pay the price of my past anguish :
> Beware, O cruel fair, how you smile on me,
> 'Twas a kind look of yours, that has undone me.
>
> Love has in store for me one happy minute,
> And she will end my pain, who did begin it ;
> Then no day void of bliss, of pleasure, leaving,
> Ages shall slide away without perceiving :
> Cupid shall guard the door, the more to please us,
> And keep out time and death, when they would seize us :
> Time and death shall depart, and say in flying
> Love has found out a way to live by dying.

Last of all the long list came *Love Triumphant*, a
tragi-comedy, in 1694, which failed completely ; why,
it is not very easy to say.   It is probable that these
four plays and the opera did not by any means requite
Dryden for his trouble in writing them.   The average
literary worth of them is, however, superior to that of
his earlier dramas.   The remarkable thing, indeed, about
this portion of his work is not that it is not better, but
that it is so good.   He can scarcely be said to have
had *la tête dramatique*, and yet in the *Conquest of
Granada*, in *Marriage à la Mode*, in *Aurengzebe*, in *All*

for Love, in the *Spanish Friar*, in *Don Sebastian*, and in *Amphitryon* he produced plays which are certainly worthy of no little admiration. For the rest, save in isolated scenes and characters, little can be said, and even those just specified have to be praised with not a little allowance.

Nevertheless, great as are the drawbacks of these plays, their position in the history of English dramatic literature is still a high and remarkable one. It was Dryden who, if he for the moment headed the desertion of the purely English style of drama, authoritatively and finally ordered and initiated the return to a saner tradition. Even in his period of aberration he produced on his faulty plan such work as few other men have produced on the best plans yet elaborated. The reader who, ignorant of the English heroic play, goes to Dryden for information about it, may be surprised and shocked at its inferiority to the drama of the great masters. But he who goes to it knowing the contemporary work of Davenant and Boyle, of Howard and Settle, will rather wonder at the unmatched literary faculty which from such data could evolve such a result. The one play in which he gave himself the reins remains, as far as it appears to me, the only play, with the exception of *Venice Preserved*, which was written so as to be thoroughly worth reading now for 150, I had almost said for 200 years. The *Mourning Bride* and the *Fair Penitent* are worthless by the side of it, and to them may be added at one sweep every tragedy written during the whole eighteenth century. Since the beginning of the nineteenth we have indeed improved the poetical standard of this most difficult not to say hopeless form of composition; but at the same time we have in general lowered the dramatic standard. Half the best plays

written since the year 1800 have been avowedly written
with hardly a thought of being acted; I should be sorry
to say how many of the other half have either failed to be
acted at all, or having been acted have proved dead
failures.   Now Dryden did so far manage to conciliate the
gifts of the play-wright and the poet, that he produced
work which was good poetry and good acting material.
It is idle to dispute the deserts of his success, the fact
remains.

Most, however, of his numerous hostile critics would
confess and avoid the tragedies, and would concentrate
their attention on the comedies.   It is impossible to help,
in part, imitating and transferring their tactics.   No
apology for the offensive characteristics of these productions is possible, and, if it were possible, I for one have
no care to attempt it.   The coarseness of Dryden's plays
is unpardonable.   It does not come under any of the
numerous categories of excuse which can be devised for
other offenders in the same kind.   It is deliberate, it is
unnecessary, it is a positive defect in art.   When the
culprit in his otherwise dignified and not unsuccessful
confiteor to Collier, endeavours to shield himself by the
example of the elder dramatists, the shield is seen at
once, and what is more we know that he must have seen
it himself, to be a mere shield of paper.   But in truth the
heaviest punishment that Dryden could possibly have
suffered, the punishment which Diderot has indicated as
inevitably imminent on this particular offence, has come
upon him.   The fouler parts of his work have simply
ceased to be read, and his most thorough defenders can
only read them for the purpose of appreciation and defence
at the price of being queasy and qualmish.   He has exposed his legs to the arrows of any criticaster who chooses

to aim at him, and the criticasters have not failed to jump
at the chance of so noble a quarry. Yet I, for my part,
shall still maintain that the merits of Dryden's comedies
are by no means inconsiderable ; indeed, that when Shakespeare, and Jonson, and Fletcher, and Etherege, and
Wycherley, and Congreve, and Vanbrugh, and Sheridan
have been put aside, he has few superiors. The unfailing
thoroughness with which he did every description of
literary work has accompanied him even here, where he
worked according to his own confession against the grain,
and where he was less gifted by nature than scores of
other facile workers who could be named. The one
situation which he could manage has been already indicated,
and it is surely not a thing to be wholly neglected that his
handlings of this situation undoubtedly preceded and probably suggested the crowning triumph of English comedy,
the sublime apotheosis of the coquette in Millamant. To
produce that triumph Dryden himself was indeed unable.
But from sheer literary skill (the dominant faculty in him)
he produced in Doralice, and in Melantha, and in Florimel, something not wholly unlike it. So, too, in the
central figure of the *Spanish Friar* he achieved in the same
way, by sheer literary faculty and by the skilful manipula-
tion of his predecessors, something like an independent
and an original creation. The one disqualification under
which Dryden laboured, the disqualification to create a
character, would have been in any lesser man a hopeless
bar even to the most moderate dramatic success. But the
superhuman degree in which he possessed the other and
strictly literary gift of adoption and arrangement, almost
supplied the place of what was wanting, and almost made
him the equal of the more facile makers. So close was
his study, so untiring his experiments, so sure his com-

mand, by dint of practice, of language, and metre, and
situation that he could, like the magicians of Egypt, make
serpents almost like, or quite like those of the true
dramatic Moses. Shakespeare's serpents have eaten his up
in time, and the retribution is just, but the credit of the
original feat is hardly the less for that.   In short all,
or almost all, Dryden's dramatic work is a *tour de force*,
but then it is such a *tour de force* as the world has hardly
elsewhere seen.   He was "bade to toil on to make them
sport," and he obeyed the bidding with perhaps less reluc-
tance than he should have shown.   But he managed, as
genius always does manage, to turn the hack-work into
a possession for ever here and there.   Unluckily it was
only here and there, and no more can be claimed for it by
any rational critic.

The subject of Dryden's prose work is intimately connected with that of his dramatic performances.   Had it
not been for the interest he felt in matters dramatic, he
might never have ventured into anything longer than a
preface ; and his prefaces would certainly have lacked the
remarkable interest in the history of style and in the history of criticism which they now possess.   At the time
when he first began to write, the accepted prose style of
English was in much greater need of reform and reinforce-
ment than the accepted poetical style ; or, to speak more
properly, there was no accepted prose style at all.   Great
masters—Bacon, Hooker, Clarendon, Milton, Taylor,
Hobbes, Bunyan, and some others—may be quoted from
the first two-thirds of the seventeenth century ; but their
excellences, like the excellences of the writers of French
prose somewhat earlier, were almost wholly individual, and
provided in no way a model whereby the average writer
might form himself for average purposes.   Now, prose is

above all things the instrument of the average purpose.
Poetry is more or less intolerable if it be not intrinsically
and peculiarly good ; prose is the necessary vehicle of
thought. Up to Dryden's time no such generally available
vehicle had been attempted or achieved by any one.
Clarendon had shown how genius can make the best of
the worst style, which from any general point of view his
must probably be pronounced to be. In his hands it is
alternately delightful or tolerable : in the hands of any-
body else it would be simply frightful. His parenthesis,
his asides, his endless involutions of phrase and thought
save themselves as if by miracle, and certainly could not
be trusted so to save themselves in any less favoured hands.
Bacon and Hooker, the former in an ornate, the latter in a
simple style, reproduce classical constructions and forms in
English. Taylor and Milton write poetry in prose. Quaintness and picturesque matter justify, and more than justify,
Fuller and Browne. Bunyan puts the vernacular into print
with a sublime assurance and success. Hobbes, casting off
all ornament and all pretence of ornament, clothes his
naked strength in the simplest garment of words competent
to cover its nakedness. But none of these had elaborated,
or aimed at elaborating, a style suited for everyday use—
for the essayist and the pamphleteer, the preacher and the
lay orator, the historian and the critic. This was what
Dryden did with little assistance from any forerunner, if
it were not Tillotson, to whom, as we know from Congreve, he acknowledged his indebtedness. But Tillotson
was not a much older man than Dryden himself, and at
least when the latter began to write prose, his work was
neither bulky nor particularly famous. Nor in reading
Tillotson, though it is clear that he and Dryden were in
some sort working on the same lines, is it possible to trace

much indebtedness on the part of the poet. The sometime archbishop's sermons are excellent in their combina-
tion of simplicity with a certain grace, but they are much
less remarkable than Dryden's own work for the union of
the two. The great fault of the elders had been, first, the
inordinate length of their sentences; secondly—and this
was rather a cause of the first fault than an additional
error—their indulgence in parenthetic quotations, borrowed
arguments, and other strengtheners of the position of the
man who has to rely on authority; thirdly, the danger to
which they were always exposed, of slipping into clumsy
classicisms on one side, or inelegant vernacular on the
other. Dryden avoided all these faults, though his avoidance was not a matter of a day or a year, nor was it, as
far as can be made out, altogether an avoidance of malice
prepense. Accident favoured him in exactly the reverse
way to that in which it had favoured the reformer of
French prose half a century or so before. Balzac had
nothing to say, and therefore was extremely careful and
exquisite in his manner of saying it. Dryden had a great
deal to say, and said it in the plain, straightforward fashion
which was of all things most likely to be useful for the
formation of a workman-like prose style in English.

The influences of the post-Restoration period which, by
their working, produced the splendid variety and efficiency
of prose in the eighteenth century—the century, *par excellence*, of prose in English—were naturally numerous;
but there were four which had an influence far surpassing
that of the rest. These four were the influences of the
pulpit, of political discussion, of miscellaneous writing—
partly fictitious, partly discursive—and lastly, of literary
criticism. In this last Dryden himself was the great
authority of the period, and for many years it was in this

form that he at once exercised himself and educated his
age in the matter of prose writing. Accident, and the
circumstances of the time, helped to give him a considerable audience and an influence of great width, the critical
spirit being extensively diffused at the time. This critical
spirit was to a great extent a reflection of that which,
beginning with Malherbe and continuing with the institution and regulation of the Academy, had for some time
been remarkable in France. Not long after the Restoration one of the subtlest and most accomplished of all
French critics took up his residence in England, and gave
further impulse to the fashion which Charles himself and
many other cavaliers had already picked up. Saint
Evremond lived in England for some forty years, and
during the greater part of that time was an oracle of the
younger men of wit and pleasure about London. Now
Saint Evremond was a remarkable instance of that rare
animal, the born critic ; even now-a-days his critical dicta
are worthy of all attention. He had a kind of critical
intuition, which is to be paralleled only by the historical
and scientific intuition which some of the greatest historians and men of science have had. With national and
characteristic indolence he never gave himself the trouble to
learn English properly, and it is doubtful whether he could
have read a single English play. Yet his critical remarks on
some English poets, not borrowed from his friends, but
constructed from their remarks, as a clever counsel would
construct a pleading out of the information furnished him,
are extraordinarily acute and accurate. The relish for
literary discussion which Saint Evremond shows was no
peculiarity of his, though he had it in super-eminent measure. It was fashionable in France, and he helped to make
it fashionable in England.

I have seen this style of criticism dismissed contemptu-
ously as "trifling;" but this is only an instance of the
strange power of reaction. Because for many years the
plan of criticising by rule and line was almost exclusively
pursued, and, as happens in the case of almost all exclu-
sive pursuits, was followed too far, it seems to some people
now-a-days, that criticism ought to be confined to the expression in more or less elegant language of the feelings of
admiration or dislike which the subject criticised may excite
in the critic's mind. The critic ought to give this impression, but he ought not to leave the other task unattempted,
and the result of leaving it unattempted is to be found in the
loose and haphazard judgments which now too often compose what is called criticism. The criticism of the Gallic
School, which Dryden and Saint Evremond helped so
much to naturalize in England, was at least not afraid of
giving a reason for the faith that was in it. The critics
strove to examine the abstract value of this or that literary
form, the propriety of this or that mode of expression,
the limits to be imposed on the choice and disposition of
this or that subject. No doubt this often resulted in
looking merely at the stopwatch, as Sterne's famous phrase
has it. But it often resulted in something better, and it
at least produced something like reasonable uniformity of
judgment.

Dryden's criticisms took, as a rule, the form of prefaces
to his plays, and the reading of the play ensured, to some
considerable extent, the reading of the preface. Probably
the pattern may be found in Corneille's *Examens*. Nor
must it be forgotten that the questions attacked in these
disquisitions were of real interest at the time to a large
number of persons; to a very much larger number rela-
tively, perhaps even to a much larger number absolutely,

than would now be the case. The first instance of a considerable piece of prose written by Dryden was not indeed
a preface, though it was of the nature of one. The *Essay
on Dramatic Poesy* was written, according to its own showing, in the summer of 1665, and published two or three
years later. It takes the form of a dialogue between in-
terlocutors, who are sufficiently identified with Dorset,
Sedley, Sir Robert Howard, and Dryden himself. The
argument turns on various questions of comparison between
classical French and English dramas, and especially between English dramas of the old and of the newer type,
the latter of which Dryden defends. It is noticeable,
however, that this very essay contained one of the best
worded and best thought out of the author's many pane-
gyrics upon Shakespeare. Viewed simply from the point
of view of style this performance exhibits Dryden as
already a considerable master of prose, though, so far as
we know, he had had no practice in it beyond a few
Prefaces and Dedications, if we except the unacknowledged
hackwork which he is sometimes said to have performed
for the bookseller Herringman. There is still something
of the older, lengthy sentence, and of the tendency to
elongate it by joint on joint as fresh thoughts recur to the
writer. But these elongations rarely sacrifice clearness,
and there is an almost total absence on the one hand of
the cumbrous classical constructions of the elders; on
the other, of the quaint colloquialisms which generally
make their appearance when this more ambitious style is
discarded. The Essay was quickly followed by a kind
of reply from Sir Robert Howard, and Dryden made a
somewhat sharp rejoinder to his brother-in-law in the
defence of the Essay which he prefixed to his play of
The Indian Emperor. He was evidently very angry with

Sir Robert, who had indeed somewhat justified Shadwell's
caricature of him as " Sir Positive At-All," and this anger
is not without effects on the style of the defence. Its
sentences are sharper, shorter, more briskly and flippantly
moulded than those of the Essay. Indeed, about this time,
the time of his greatest prosperity, Dryden seems to have
passed, somewhat late in life, through a period of flip-
pancy. He was, for a few years, decidedly prosperous,
and his familiarity with men of rank and position seems
a little to have turned his head. It was at this time, and
at this time only, that he spoke disrespectfully of his great
predecessors, and insinuated, in a manner which I fear
must be called snobbish, that his own familiarity with
such models of taste and deportment as Rochester, put him
in a very superior position for the drawing of character,
to such humble and home-keeping folks as the old dramatists. These prefaces and dedications, however, even
where their matter is scarcely satisfactory, show an ever-
growing command of prose style, and, very soon, the resi-
piscence of Dryden's judgment and the result of his
recently renewed study of the older writers. The Preface to
All for Love, though short and more familiar in style than
the earlier work is of excellent quality, and the same may
be said of those to *Troïlus and Cressida* and the *Spanish
Friar*, the latter of which is especially characteristic, and
contains some striking remarks on the old dramatists. The
great poetical works of the period between 1680 and 1687
are also attended by prose introductions, and some of these
are exceedingly well done. The *Epistle to the Whigs*,
which forms the preface to the *Medal*, is a piece of political writing such as there had been hitherto but very little
in English, and it was admirably followed up by the *Vin-
dication of the Duke of Guise*. On the other hand, the

preface to *Religio Laici*, though partly also polemical, is a
model of what may be called the expository style. Dryden
obtained no great credit for his controversy with Stillingfleet, his *Life of St. Francis Xavier*, or his *History of
the League*, all of which were directly or indirectly controversial, and concerned with the political events of the
time. As his lengthiest prose works, however, they can
hardly be passed over without notice.

The Revolution, in throwing Dryden back upon purely
literary pursuits, did him no more harm in the way of
prose than of poetical composition. Not a few of his
Translations have prose prefaces of peculiar excellence
prefixed. The sketch of Satire which forms the preface to
the *Juvenal*, is one of the best of its author's performances.
The *Æneid* is introduced by an admirable dedication to
Mulgrave; but the essay on the *Georgics*, though it is not
indeed Dryden's own, is almost more interesting in this
connexion than if it were—for this essay came from the pen
of no less a person than Addison, then a young man of five-
and-twenty, and it enables us to judge of the indebtedness
of the Queen Anne men to Dryden in prose as well as in
poetry. It would be a keen critic who, knowing Addison
only from the *Spectator*, could detect his hand in this performance. But it does not require much keenness in any
one who knows Dryden's prose and Addison's, to trace
the link of connexion which this piece affords. It lies
much nearer to the former than the latter, and it shows
clearly how the writer must have studied those "prefaces of
Dryden" which Swift chose to sneer at. As in poetry, however, so in prose, Dryden's best, or almost his best work,
was his last. The dedication of the *Fables* to the Duke
of Ormond is the last and the most splendid of his many
pieces of polished flattery. The preface which follows

it is the last, and one of the best examples of his literary
criticism.

It has been justly observed of Dryden's prose style that
it is, for the style of so distinguished a writer, singularly
destitute of mannerism. If we father any particular
piece upon him without knowing it to be his, it is not,
as in the case of most writers, because of some obvious
trick of arrangement or phraseology. The truth is, or
at least the probability, that Dryden had no thought of
inventing or practising a definite prose style, though he
had more than once a very definite intention in his
practice of matters poetical. Poetry was with him, as
indeed it should be, an end in itself ; prose, as perhaps it
should also be for the most part, only a means to an end.
He wanted from time to time to express his ideas on
certain points that interested him; to answer accusations
which he thought unjust ; to propitiate powerful patrons ;
sometimes, perhaps, merely to discharge commissions with
which he had been intrusted. He found no good instrument ready to his hand for these purposes, and so, with
that union of the practical and literary spirit which distinguished him so strongly, he set to work to make one.
But he had no special predilection for the instrument,
except in so far as it served its turn, and he had therefore
no object in preserving any special peculiarities in it
except for the same reason. His poetical and dramatic
practice, and the studies which that practice implied, provided him with an ample vocabulary, a strong, terse
method of expression, and a dislike to archaism, vulgarity,
or want of clearness. He therefore let his words arrange
themselves pretty much as they would, and probably saw
no object in such devices as the balancing of one part of
a sentence by another, which attracted so many of his

K

successors. The long sentence with its involved clauses
was contrary to his habit of thought, and would have
interfered with his chief objects—clearness and precision.
Therefore he, in the main, discarded it, yet if at any time a
long and somewhat complicated sentence seemed to him
to be appropriate he did not hesitate to write one. Slip-
shod diction and cant vulgarities revolted his notions of
correctness and elegance, and therefore he seldom uses
them; yet there are not very many writers in whom
colloquialisms occasionally occur with happier effect. If
a fault is to be found with his style it probably lies in a
certain abuse of figures and of quotation, for both of which
his strong tincture of the characteristics of the first half of
the century may be responsible, while the former at least
is natural to a poet. Yet on the whole his style, if compared either with Hooker and Clarendon, Bacon and
Milton on the one hand, or with Addison, and still more
the later eighteenth century writers on the other, is a distinctly plain and homely style. It is not so vernacular as
Bunyan or Defoe, and not quite so perfect in simplicity as
Swift. Yet with the work of these three writers it stands
at the head of the plainer English prose styles, possessing
at the same time a capacity of magnificence to which the
others cannot pretend. As there is no original narrative
of any length from Dryden's hand in prose, it is difficult to
say whether he could have discharged satisfactorily this
part of the prose-writer's functions. The *Life of Xavier* is
good, but not of the best. For almost any other function,
however, the style seems to be well adapted.

Now this, it must be remembered, was the great want
of the day in matter of prose style—a style, namely, that
should be generally flexible and capable of adaptation,
not merely to the purposes of the erudite and ambitious,

but to any purpose for which it might be required, and in which the vernacular and the literary elements should be properly blended and adjusted. It is scarcely too much to say that if, as some critics have inclined to think, the influence of Dryden tended to narrow the sphere and cramp the efforts of English poetry, it tended equally to enlarge the sphere and develope the energies of English prose. It has often been noticed that poets, when they have any faculty for prose writing, are among the best of prose writers, and of no one is this more true than it is of Dryden.

Set prose passages of laboured excellence are not very common with Dryden. But the two following, the first being the famous character of Shakespeare from the *Essay on Dramatic Poesy*, the second an extract from the preface to the *Fables*, will give some idea of his style at periods separated by more than thirty years. The one was his first work of finished prose, the other his last :—

As Neander was beginning to examine "The Silent Woman," Eugenius, earnestly regarding him; I beseech you, Neander, said he, gratify the company, and me in particular, so far, as before you speak of the play, to give us a character of the author; and tell us frankly your opinion, whether you do not think all writers, both French and English, ought to give place to him. I fear, replied Neander, that in obeying your commands I shall draw some envy on myself. Besides, in performing them, it will be first necessary to speak somewhat of Shakespeare and Fletcher, his rivals in poesy; and one of them, in my opinion, at least his equal, perhaps his superior. To begin then with Shakespeare. He was the man who of all modern, and perhaps ancient poets, had the largest and most comprehensive soul. All the images of nature were still present to him, and he drew them not laboriously, but luckily : when he describes anything, you more than see it, you feel it too. Those who accuse him to have wanted learning, give him

the greater commendation : he was naturally learned ; he
needed not the spectacles of books to read nature ; he looked
inwards, and found her there. I cannot say he is everywhere
alike; were he so, I should do him injury to compare him with
the greatest of mankind. He is many times flat, insipid ; his
comick wit degenerating into clenches, his serious swelling into
bombast. But he is always great, when some great occasion is
presented to him ; no man can say he ever had a fit subject for
his wit, and did not then raise himself as high above the rest of
poets,

> Quantum lenta solent inter viburna cupressi.

The consideration of this made Mr. Hales of Eton say, that
there was no subject of which any poet ever writ but he would
produce it much better done in Shakespeare ; and however
others are now generally preferred before him, yet the age
wherein he lived, which had contemporaries with him, Fletcher
and Jonson, never equalled them to him in their esteem : and
in the last king's court, when Ben's reputation was at highest,
Sir John Suckling, and with him the greater part of the
courtiers, set our Shakespeare far above him.

As for the religion of our poet,[1] he seems to have some little
bias towards the opinions of Wickliffe, after John of Gaunt, his
patron ; somewhat of which appears in the "Tale of Pierce
Plowman," yet I cannot blame him for inveighing so sharply
against the vices of the clergy in his age : their pride, their
ambition, their pomp, their avarice, their worldly interest, deserved the lashes which he gave them, both in that, and in
most of his Canterbury Tales. Neither has his contemporary,
Boccace, spared them. Yet both those poets lived in much
esteem with good and holy men in orders ; for the scandal
which is given by particular priests, reflects not on the sacred
function. Chaucer's Monk, his Canon, and his Friar, took not
from the character of his Good Parson. A satirical poet is the
check of the laymen on bad priests. We are only to take care

----

[1] Chaucer.

that we involve not the innocent with the guilty in the same
condemnation. The good cannot be too much honoured, nor
the bad too coarsely used; for the corruption of the best
becomes the worst. When a clergyman is whipped, his
gown is first taken off, by which the dignity of his order
is secured. If he be wrongfully accused, he has his action of
slander; and it is at the poet's peril, if he transgress the
law. But they will tell us, that all kind of satire, though
never so well deserved by particular priests, yet brings the
whole order into contempt. Is then the peerage of England
anything dishonoured, when a peer suffers for his treason?
If he be libelled, or any way defamed, he has his scandalum
magnatum to punish the offender. They who use this kind of
argument, seem to be conscious to themselves of somewhat
which has deserved the poet's lash, and are less concerned for
their publick capacity, than for their private; at least there is
pride at the bottom of their reasoning. If the faults of men in
orders are only to be judged among themselves, they are all in
some sort parties; for, since they say the honour of their order
is concerned in every member of it, how can we be sure that
they will be impartial judges? How far I may be allowed to
speak my opinion in this case, I know not; but I am sure a
dispute of this nature caused mischief in abundance betwixt a
King of England and an Archbishop of Canterbury; one standing up for the laws of his land, and the other for the honour
(as he called it) of God's church; which ended in the murder of
the Prelate, and in the whipping of his Majesty from post to
pillar for his penance. The learned and ingenious Dr. Drake
has saved me the labour of enquiring into the esteem and re-
verence which the priests have had of old; and I would rather
extend than diminish any part of it: yet I must needs say, that
when a priest provokes me without any occasion given him, I
have no reason, unless it be the charity of a Christian, to forgive
him: *prior læsit* is justification sufficient in the civil law. If
I answer him in his own language, self-defence, I am sure,
must be allowed me; and if I carry it farther, even to a sharp
recrimination, somewhat may be indulged to human frailty.
Yet my resentment has not wrought so far, but that I have

followed Chaucer in his character of a holy man, and have enlarged on that subject with some pleasure ; reserving to myself
the right, if I shall think fit hereafter, to describe another sort
of priests, such as are more easily to be found than the Good
Parson ; such as have given the last blow to Christianity in
this age, by a practice so contrary to their doctrine.   But this
will keep cold till another time.   In the mean while I take up
Chaucer where I left him.

These must suffice for examples of the matter as well
as of the manner of the literary criticism which forms the
chief and certainly the most valuable part of Dryden's
prose works.   The great value of that criticism consists
in its extremely appreciative character, and in its constant
connexion with the poet's own constructive work.   There
is much in it which might seem to expose Dryden to the
charge of inconsistency.   But the truth is, that his literary
opinions were in a perpetual state of progress, and therefore of apparent flux.   Sometimes he wrote with defective
knowledge, sometimes, though not often, without thinking
the subject out, sometimes (and this very often) with a
certain one-sidedness of view having reference rather to
the bearing of the point on experiments he was then
trying or about to try, than to any more abstract con-
siderations.   He never aimed at paradox for its own sake,
but he never shrank from it ; and on the whole his
criticisms, though perhaps nowadays they appeal rather to
the expert and the student than to the general reader, are at
least as interesting for their matter as for their form.   The
importance of the study of that form in the cultivation of
a robust English style has never been denied.

CHAPTER VII.

PERIOD OF TRANSLATION.

It is in many cases a decidedly difficult problem to settle
the exact influence which any writer's life and circumstances have upon his literary performances and career.
Although there are probably few natures so absolutely
self-sufficing and so imperial in their individuality that
they take no imprint from the form and pressure of the
time, the exact force which that pressure exercises is
nearly always very hard to calculate. In the case of
Dryden, however, the difficulty is fortunately minimized.
There was never, it may safely be said, so great a writer
who was so thoroughly occasional in the character of
his greatness. The one thing which to all appearance
he could not do, was to originate a theme. His second
best play, according to the general judgment, his best as
I venture to think, is built, with an audacity to which
only great genius or great folly could lead, on the lines of
Shakespeare. His longest and most ambitious poem follows
with a surprising faithfulness the lines of Chaucer. His most
effective piece of tragic description is a versified paraphrase
—the most magnificent paraphrase perhaps ever written
—of the prose of Boccaccio. Even in his splendid satires
he is rarely successful, unless he has what is called in
modern literary slang a very definite " peg " given him to

hang his verse upon. *Absalom and Achitophel* is little
more than a loosely connected string of characters, each
owing no doubt something, and what is more, a great deal
to the poet, but originally given to, and not invented by
him. No fashion of poetry can be farther aloof from
Dryden's than that which, as in the case of Shelley, spins
great poems purely out of its own brain. His strong and
powerful mind could grind the corn supplied to it into
the finest flour, but the corn must always be supplied.
The exquisite perfection of his smaller lyrics forbids us to
set this down as in any sense a drawback. It was rather
a strong inclination to the one office than an incapacity
for the other. What is more to the purpose, this peculiarity is very closely connected with Dryden's fitness for
the position which he held. The man who is to control
the peaceable revolution of a literature, who is to shape
a language to new uses, and help writers for a century
after his death to vocabulary, rhythm, and style, in
prose as well as in verse, is perhaps all the better off for
not being too spontaneous or original in his choice of
subjects. But however this may be, there is no doubt
that outward circumstances always had a great, and the
greatest influence upon the development of Dryden's
genius. There was in some respects a quality about this
genius for which it would be hard to find an appropriate
name. To call such a mind and such a talent as Dryden's
parasitic would be ridiculous. Yet in any lesser man the
same characteristics would undoubtedly receive that appel-
lation. It seems always to have been, if not necessary,
at any rate satisfactory to him, to follow some lines which
had been already laid down, to accept a departure from
some previous work, to match himself closely with some
existing performance. It appears almost as if, in his ex-

traordinary care for the manner of his poetical work, he
felt it an advantage to be relieved of much trouble about
the matter. The accusations of plagiarism which his
frantic enemies constantly brought against him were,
in any discreditable sense, as idle as accusations of
plagiarism usually are ; but they had considerably more
foundation in literal fact than is usual with such accusations. He had a habit of catching up phrases sometimes
from the works of men to whom he was anything but
complimentary, and inserting them, much improved it
is true for the most part, in his own work. I have come
across a curious instance of this, which I do not remember
to have seen anywhere noticed. One of the most morti-
fying incidents in Dryden's literary career was the already
mentioned composition by his rival, though not exactly
enemy, Crowne, of the Masque of *Calisto*. There seems
to be little doubt, though the evidence is not entirely
conclusive, that Crowne's share in this work was due to
Rochester, who afterwards made himself obnoxious to
Dryden's wrath in a still more unpardonable manner.
Under these circumstances we certainly should not expect
to find Dryden borrowing from *Calisto*. Yet a whole
line in *Macflecknoe*, "The fair Augusta much to fears
inclined," is taken, with the addition of the adjective and
the adverb, from a song of Crowne's : " Augusta is to fears
inclined." This temperament made the work of translation one peculiarly suitable to Dryden. He had, as early
as 1684, included several translations in his first volume
of Miscellanies, and he soon perceived that there was
plenty of demand for more of the same ware. Except his
great editor, it is doubtful whether any man of letters ever
knew the public taste better than Dryden. The call
for translations of the ancients was quite natural and

intelligible. Direct classical study was considerably on
the wane. So far indeed as one sex was concerned, it had
practically gone out of fashion altogether, and women
of the accomplishments of Lady Jane Grey or Queen
Elizabeth were now thought monsters. Even as regards
men, a much smaller proportion of the upper classes were
able to read the classics in the original than had once been
the case. Business, court life, employment in a standing
army and navy, and many other distractions called men
early away from their studies. Yet the interest felt, or
supposed to be felt in classical literature, was at least as
great as ever. The classics were still considered as literary
models and patterns ; and the famous controversy between
the ancients and the moderns which arose about this time,
helped to inspire a desire for some acquaintance with the
former in the easy fashionable verse which Dryden had
himself created. In 1693 he gave to the world the whole
of Persius and much of Juvenal, the latter being com-
pleted by his sons and some friends. In the same year
some more versions of Ovid and a little of Homer appeared ; and in 1693 also his greatest work of translation,
the Virgil, was begun. This was the only one of Dryden's
works for which he received not wholly inadequate remuneration, and this remuneration was attained chiefly by the
method of subscription. Besides these authors, his translations include extracts from Theocritus and Lucretius, a very
few Odes of Horace, and a considerable portion of the
Metamorphoses of Ovid, which appeared last of all in the
well-known volume of *Fables*. The merits and peculiarities of Dryden's translation are easily estimated. It
has been excellently remarked in the Preface of a recent
prose translation of the Odyssey, that there can be no
final translation of Homer, because the taste and literary

habits of each age demand different qualities in poetry. There is no need to limit this remark to Homer, or indeed to poetry. The work of the translator is to bridge over the interval between his author and his public, and therefore the construction and character of the bridge must necessarily differ, according to the instruction and demands of the public. Dryden could not give exact accuracy, though he was by no means such a bad scholar as Pope. But his public did not want exact accuracy, and would not have been grateful for it. He did not—whether he was or was not able—give them classical flavour and local colour, but for these they would have been still less grateful. What they wanted, and what he could give them as no other man then living could, was the matter of the original, tolerably unadulterated, and dressed up in the splendid diction and nervous verse which he had himself taught them to love. The parallel between the characteristics of the translation and the simple device whereby Jacob Tonson strove to propitiate the ruling powers in the illustrations to the *Virgil* is indeed obvious enough. Those illustrations displayed "old Nassau's hook-nosed head on pious Æneas' shoulders." The text itself displayed the head of Dryden on the shoulders of Virgil.

Even before the Miscellany of 1684, translations from Dryden's hands had been published. There appeared in 1680 a version of Ovid's *Heroides*, to which he gave a preface and a translation of two epistles, besides collaborating with Mulgrave in a third. The preface contains some good criticism of Ovid, and a defence of the manner of translation which with little change Dryden himself constantly employed. This he defines as being equally remote from verbal fidelity and from mere imitation. He

also lays down a canon as to the necessary equipment of
a translator, which, if it could be despotically enforced,
would be a remarkable boon to reviewers. " No man is
capable of translating poetry, who, besides a genius to that
art, is not a master both of his author's language and of
his own. Nor must we understand the language only of
the poet, but his particular turn of thoughts and expressions, which are the characters that distinguish, and
as it were individuate him from all other writers." These
first translations are interesting because they are the first,
and for the sake of contrast with the later and more
perfect work of the same kind. In some respects Ovid
was an unfortunate author for Dryden to select, because
his peculiarities tempted a relapse into the faults of the
heroic-play style. But, on the other hand, Dryden's
practice in the heroic play fitted him very well to translate
Ovid. A few lines from the close of *Canace to Macareus*
may be given as an instance,—

> And now appeared the messenger of death;
> Sad were his looks, and scarce he drew his breath,
> To say, "Your father sends you " (with that word
> His trembling hands presented me a sword;)
> " Your father sends you this; and lets you know,
> That your own crimes the use of it will show."
> Too well I know the sense those words impart;
> His present shall be treasured in my heart.
> Are these the nuptial gifts a bride receives?
> And this the fatal dower a father gives?
> Thou God of marriage, shun thy own disgrace,
> And take thy torch from this detested place!
> Instead of that, let furies light their brands,
> And fire my pile with their infernal hands!
> With happier fortune may my sisters wed,
> Warned by the dire example of the dead.
> For thee, poor babe, what crime could they pretend?
> How could thy infant innocence offend?

> A guilt there was ; but, oh, that guilt was mine !
> Thou suffer'st for a sin that was not thine.
> Thy mother's grief and crime ! but just enjoyed,
> Shewn to my sight, and born to be destroyed !
> Unhappy offspring of my teeming womb !
> Dragged headlong from thy cradle to thy tomb !
> Thy unoffending life I could not save,
> Nor weeping could I follow to thy grave ;
> Nor on thy tomb could offer my shorn hair,
> Nor shew the grief which tender mothers bear.
> Yet long thou shalt not from my arms be lost ;
> For soon I will o'ertake thy infant ghost.
> But thou, my love, and now my love's despair,
> Perform his funerals with paternal care ;
> His scattered limbs with my dead body burn,
> And once more join us in the pious urn.
> If on my wounded breast thou droppest a tear,
> Think for whose sake my breast that wound did bear ;
> And faithfully my last desires fulfil,
> As I perform my cruel father's will.

The Miscellanies of 1684 and 1685 contained a considerable number of translations from many different
authors, and those of 1693 and 1694 added yet more.
Altogether, besides Ovid and Virgil, specimens of Horace,
Homer, Theocritus, and Lucretius are in these translations,
while the more ambitious and complete versions of Juvenal
and Virgil swell the total (in Scott's edition) to four
volumes, containing perhaps some 30,000 lines.

It could hardly be expected that in translating authors
of such different characters, and requiring in a poetical
translator so many different gifts, Dryden should be
altogether and equally successful. The *Juvenal* and the
Virgil deserve separate notice ; the others may be briefly
reviewed. All of them are, according to the general
conception of translation which Dryden had formed,
decidedly loose, and by no means adhere to the original.

Indeed, Dryden not unfrequently inserts whole lines and
passages of his own, a proceeding scarcely to be reconciled
with the just-mentioned conception. On the whole he
is perhaps most successful with Ovid. The versions of
Horace are few, and by no means excessively Horatian,
but they are almost all good poems in Dryden's statelier
rhythm. The version into a kind of Pindaric of the
twenty-ninth ode of the third book is particularly good,
and contains the well-known paraphrase of *resigno quæ
dedit* (" I puff the prostitute away "), which was such a
favourite with Thackeray that he puts it into the mouth,
if I remember rightly, of more than one of his characters.
Indeed, the three last stanzas of this are well worth
quotation,—

VIII.

Happy the man, and happy he alone,
He, who can call to-day his own;
He who, secure within, can say,
To-morrow do thy worst, for I have lived to-day;
Be fair, or foul, or rain, or shine,
The joys I have possessed, in spite of fate, are mine;
Not heaven itself upon the past has power,
But what has been, has been, and I have had my hour.

IX.

Fortune, that with malicious joy
    Does man, her slave, oppress,
Proud of her office to destroy,
    Is seldom pleased to bless:
Still various and unconstant still,
But with an inclination to be ill,
Promotes, degrades, delights in strife,
And makes a lottery of life.
I can enjoy her while she's kind;
But when she dances in the wind,
And shakes the wings and will not stay,

I puff the prostitute away :
The little or the much she gave, is quietly resigned ;
Content with poverty, my soul I arm,
And virtue, though in rags, will keep me warm.

x.

What is't to me,
Who never sail in her unfaithful sea,
If storms arise and clouds grow black,
If the mast split, and threaten wreck ?
Then let the greedy merchant fear
   For his ill-gotten gain ;
And pray to gods that will not hear,
While the debating winds and billows bear
   His wealth into the main.
For me, secure from fortune's blows,
Secure of what I cannot lose,
   In my small pinnace I can sail,
Contemning all the blustering roar ;
   And running with a merry gale,
With friendly stars my safety seek,
Within some little winding creek,
   And see the storm ashore.

Least successful of all perhaps are the Theocritean
translations. The idyllic spirit was not one of the many
which would come at Dryden's call, and certain peculiarities of Theocritus, harmless enough in the original, are
accentuated and magnified in the copy in a manner by no
means pleasant. A thing more unfortunate still was the
selection made from Lucretius. No one was ever better
qualified to translate the greatest of Roman poets than
Dryden ; and had he given us the whole, it would probably
have been the best verse translation in the language. As
it is, he has done few things better than the selections
from the second and third books, but that from the fourth
has, justly or unjustly, tainted the whole in the eyes of
most critics. It reproduces only too nakedly the original

where it would be better left alone, and it fails almost
entirely even to attempt the sombre fury of sentiment, the
inexpressible agony of regret, which transfuse and redeem
that original itself. The first book of Homer and part of
the sixth were avowedly done as an experiment, and it is
difficult to be very sorry that the experiment was not pursued farther. But the versions of Ovid's *Metamorphoses*
are very good. They, however, belong more properly to
the next period, that of the *Fables*.

Dryden's *Juvenal* is not the least remarkable, and has
been in some ways among the most fortunate of his works.
It is still, if there be any such, the standard verse translation of the great Roman satirist, and this although much
of it is not Dryden's. His two elder sons assisted him in
the work, as well as some friends. But the first, third,
sixth, tenth, and sixteenth satires are his own, as well as
the whole of the *Persius*. The book was published in
1693, addressed to Dorset, with a prefatory essay or discourse on satire, which is of great interest and value. It
is somewhat discursive, as is Dryden's wont, and the erudition which it contains is, as is also his wont, anything
but invariably accurate. But it contains some precious
autobiographic information, much capital criticism, and
some of the best passages of its author's prose. He distinguishes between his own idea of satire and Juvenal's,
approaching the former to that of Horace, which, however, is scarcely a tenable position. But, as has been
sufficiently pointed out already, there are actually many and
grave differences between the satire of Dryden and that of
Juvenal. The former rarely or never even simulates
indignation ; the latter constantly and invariably expresses
it. Still the poetical resemblances between the two men
are sufficiently close to make the expectation of a

valuable version pretty confident, nor is that expectation
disappointed. For a wonder Dryden resists, for the most
part, his unhappy tendency to exaggerate the coarseness
of his subjects, and to choose their coarsest parts in
preference to others. No version of Juvenal could be
other than shocking to those accustomed only to modern
standards of literary language ; but this version is perhaps
less so than might be expected. The vigorous stamp of
Dryden's verse is, moreover, admirably suited to repre-
sent the original, and the chief fault noticeable in it—a
fault not uncommon with Dryden in translating—is an
occasional lapse into an unpoetical vernacular, with the
object, doubtless, of representing the text more vividly to
English readers. The *Persius* is in this respect better
than the *Juvenal*, though the peculiar dryness of flavour
of the singular original is scarcely retained.

It is not known exactly when Dryden first conceived
the idea of working up the scattered fragments of Vir-
gilian translation which he had as yet attempted into a
whole. The task, however, was regularly begun either at
the end of 1693 or the beginning of 1694, and it occupied
the best part of three years. A good deal of interest was
generally felt in the proceeding, and many friends helped
the poet with books or literary assistance of one kind or
another. A great deal of it, too, was written during
visits to hospitable acquaintances in the country. Much
of it was doubtless done in Northamptonshire and
Huntingdonshire, at the houses of Mrs. Creed and of
Driden of Chesterton. There is, indeed, a universally
repeated tradition that the first lines were written with a
diamond on a window in this latter mansion. The house
was pulled down some seventy years ago, and a curious
argument against the truth of the legend has been made

L

out of the fact that the pane was not preserved. Demolition, however, is not usually careful of its prey. Much
was certainly written at Denham Court, in Buckingham-
shire, the seat of Sir William Bowyer, whose gardens are
commemorated in a note on the Georgics. The seventh
book of the Æneid was done at Burleigh, Dryden having
long had some connexion with the Exeter family. He
had, it may be mentioned, always been fond of writing in
the country. Tonson, the publisher, was exceedingly
anxious that the book should be dedicated to William III.,
and Dryden speaks as if certain anticipations of gain had
been held out to him in such a case. But he was
unfalteringly determined to do nothing that would look
like an abandonment of his principles. No single person
received the honour of the dedication ; but each division
of the work was inscribed to a separate patron. The
Eclogues fell to the lot of Lord Clifford, Dryden's co-reli-
gionist, and son of the " fierce and brave " if not very high-
principled member of the Cabal to whom *Amboyna* had
been dedicated long before. The *Georgics* were inscribed
to Lord Chesterfield, a dedication which, with Dryden's
subsequent reception and acknowledgment of a present
from Chesterfield, is at least decisive against the supposed
connexion between Lady Elizabeth and the Earl having
been known to the poet. Mulgrave, now Marquis of
Normanby, had the *Æneid*. The book was published in
July, 1697, and the edition was sold off almost within the
year. Dryden speaks to his sons, who were now at Rome,
where they had employment in the Pope's household, with
great pleasure of its success. It is, in truth, a sufficiently
remarkable book. It was, no doubt, rather ironical of fate
to assign Homer to Pope, who was of all poets the least
Homeric, and Virgil to Dryden, than whom not many

poets have been more un-Virgilian. Pope would have
done the Mantuan, whom in many things he resembles,
excellently. Dryden has done him excellently too, only
that the spirit of the translation is entirely different from
that of the original. To say after Wordsworth that
Dryden "spoils" all the best passages is quite unfair. But
Wordsworth had no special faculty of criticism in the
classical languages, and was of all recorded poets the
most niggardly of praise, and the most prone to depreciation of others. Of the three parts as wholes the Georgics
are perhaps done best, the Eclogues worst, the Æneid
with most inequality. Yet the best passages of the epic
are the best, beyond all doubt, of the whole version. A
certain delicacy of touch, which Virgil especially requires,
and of which Dryden was sufficiently master in his more
original work, has often failed him here, but the bolder
and more masculine passages are represented with a great
deal of success. Those who believe, as I confess I myself believe, that all translation is unsatisfactory, and that poetical
translation of poetry is nearly impossible, must of course
always praise such work as this with a very considerable
reservation. But when that reservation is made, there
remains plenty of fairly disposable praise for this, Dryden's most considerable undertaking of a single and complete kind. The older translations have so far gone out
of general reading in England that citation is in this case
almost indispensable, as well for the purpose of showing
what Dryden actually did give his readers in this famous
book, as for that of exhibiting the progress he had made
since the *Ovid* of sixteen years before. The passage I
have chosen is the well-known opening of the descent
into hell in the sixth book, which has not many superiors
either in the original or in the version. The subject was

one that Dryden could handle well, whereas his Dido
sometimes shows traces of incongruity,—

> She said, and passed along the gloomy space ;
> The prince pursued her steps with equal pace.
> Ye realms, yet unrevealed to human sight !
> Ye gods, who rule the regions of the night !
> Ye gliding ghosts ! permit me to relate
> The mystic wonders of your silent state.
> Obscure they went through dreary shades, that led
> Along the waste dominions of the dead.
> Thus wander travellers in woods by night,
> By the moon's doubtful and malignant light,
> When Jove in dusky clouds involves the skies,
> And the faint crescent shoots by fits before their eyes.
> Just in the gate, and in the jaws of hell,
> Revengeful Cares and sullen Sorrows dwell,
> And pale Diseases and repining Age,
> Want, Fear, and Famine's unresisted rage ;
> Here Toils, and Death, and Death's half-brother Sleep,
> (Forms terrible to view) their centry keep ;
> With anxious Pleasures of a guilty mind,
> Deep Frauds before, and open Force behind ;
> The Furies' iron beds ; and Strife, that shakes
> Her hissing tresses, and unfolds her snakes.
> Full in the midst of this infernal road,
> An elm displays her dusky arms abroad :
> The god of sleep there hides his heavy head,
> And empty dreams on every leaf are spread.
> Of various forms unnumbered spectres more,
> Centaurs, and double shapes, besiege the door.
> Before the passage, horrid Hydra stands,
> And Briareus with all his hundred hands ;
> Gorgons, Geryon with his triple frame ;
> And vain Chimæra vomits empty flame.
> The chief unsheathed his shining steel, prepared,
> Though seized with sudden fear, to force the guard,
> Offering his brandished weapon at their face ;
> Had not the Sibyl stopped his eager pace,
> And told him what those empty phantoms were—
> Forms without bodies, and impassive air.

Owing to the existence of some letters to Tonson, Walsh, and others, more is known about the pecuniary side of this transaction than about most of Dryden's money affairs. Tonson was an exceedingly hard bargain-driver, and there is extant a curious letter of his, in which he complains of the number of verses he has for his money, a complaint which, as we shall see when we come to the *Fables*, was at any rate in that case grossly unjust. The book was published by subscription, as Pope's *Homer* was subsequently, but the terms were not nearly so profitable to the poet. A hundred and two five-guinea subscribers had each his arms printed at the foot of one of the hundred and two plates. Others who subscribed only two guineas merely figured in a list of names. But except a statement by Dryden in a letter that " the thirty shillings upon every book remains with me," the proportion in which the subscriptions were divided between author and publisher is unknown. He had, however, as Malone thinks, 50*l.* for each book of the *Æneid*,—as Mr. Christie and Mr. Hooper think, 50*l.* for each two books,—and no doubt there was some similar payment for the *Eclogues* and *Georgics.* Altogether Pope heard that he made 1200*l.* by the *Virgil*. Presents too were doubtless sent him by Clifford and Mul-grave, as well as by Chesterfield. But Tonson's payments were anything but satisfactory, and Lord Macaulay has extracted much evidence as to the state of the coinage from Dryden's indignant letters on the subject. At one time he complains that in some money changed for Lady Elizabeth by Tonson, " besides the clipped money there were at least forty shillings brass." Then he expects " good silver, not such as he had formerly," and will not take gold, of course because of the renewed risk of bad money in change. Then complaints are made of Tonson

for refusing subscriptions (which shows that a considerable portion of the subscription-money must have gone to
the poet), for declining to pay anything for notes, and so
on.   The most complimentary thing to Tonson in the
correspondence is the remark, " All of your trade are
sharpers, and you not more than others."   In the next
letter, however, the suspicion as to the goodness of Tonson's money returns,—" If you have any silver *which will
go*, my wife will be glad of it."   Elsewhere there is a half-
apologetic allusion to a " sharp " letter which seems not to
have been preserved.   But Dryden had confidence enough
in his publisher to make him do various pieces of fiduciary
business for him, such as to receive his rents which had
been brought up from Northamptonshire by the Towcester
carrier, to get bills to pay a suspicious watchmaker who
would not take gold, and the like.   He too was the inter-
mediary by which Dryden sent letters to his sons who
were now in Rome, and he is accused of great carelessness
and perhaps something worse in connexion with these
letters.   In another epistle we hear that " the printer is a
beast," an accusation which it is to be feared has been
repeated frequently since by impatient authors.   Afterwards, in rather Landorian style—indeed, there are resemblances more than one between the two, and Landor was
a constant admirer of Dryden—he " vows to God that if
Everingham, the printer, takes not care of this impression,
he shall never print anything more for him."   These
letters to Tonson about the *Virgil* and the *Fables* are
among the most interesting memorials of Dryden that we
possess, and, they are, with those to Mrs. Steward, almost
the only letters of his which give much personal detail.[1]

[1] As, for instance, how (he is writing from Northamptonshire)
a party of benighted strangers came in, and he had to give up his

Perhaps it is not superfluous to say that allusions in them to his wife are frequent, and show nothing either of any ill-feeling between the two, or of any neglect of household duty on her part. To one of the letters to his sons is a long postscript from Lady Elizabeth, in perhaps the most remarkable orthography that even English epistolary history has to show, but affectionate and motherly enough.

During the period which the last two chapters cover, Dryden had as usual not failed to undertake several minor and miscellaneous literary tasks. *Eleonora*, in 1692, was one of his least successful pieces in a literary point of view, but perhaps the most successful of all as a piece of journeywork. The poem is an elegy on the Countess of Abingdon : it was ordered by her husband, and paid for munificently. There are but 377 verses, and the fee was five hundred guineas, or on Tonson's method of calculation some seven or eight-and-twenty shillings a line—a rate which would have seemed to Jacob sinful, as encouraging poets to be extortionate with honest tradesmen. The piece is laboured and ill-sustained. If it deserved five hundred guineas, the Anne Killigrew ode would certainly have been cheap at five thousand. But not long afterwards a poem to Sir Godfrey Kneller, which may or may not have been exchanged for something of the other artist's craft, showed that Dryden had in no way lost his faculty of splendid flattery. Perhaps before and perhaps after this came the incomparable address to Congreve on the failure of the *Double Dealer*, which is and deserves to be one of Dryden's best-known works. Congreve and Southerne, the leading comic writer and the leading tragic writer of

bed to them, to which bed they would have gone supperless, had he not " taken a very lusty pike that day."

the younger generation, were among the principal of the
band of sons (in Ben Jonson's phrase) whom Dryden
had now gathered round him.   In one of his letters
there is a very pleasant picture of the two young men
coming out four miles to meet the coach as he returned
from one of his Northamptonshire visits, and escorting
him to his house. This was in 1695, and in the same
year Dryden brought out a prose translation of Du Fres-
noy's *Art of Painting*, with a prefatory essay called a
"Parallel of Poetry and Painting."   There is not very
much intrinsic value in this parallel, but it has an accidental interest of a curious kind.   Dryden tells us that it
occupied him for twelve mornings, and we are therefore
able to calculate his average rate of working, since neither
the matter nor the manner of the work betokens any extraordinary care, nor could it have required extraordinary re-
search.   The essay would fill between thirty and forty
pages of the size of this present.   Either in 1695 or in 1696
the poet also wrote a life of Lucian, intended to accompany
a translation of the Dialogues made by various hands.
This too, which did not appear till after the author's
death, was something of a "pot-boiler," but the character
of Dryden's prose work was amply redeemed by the
"Discourse on Epic Poetry," which was the form that
the dedication of the *Æneid* to Mulgrave took.   This is
not unworthy to rank with the "Essay on Dramatic
Poesy" and the "Discourse on Satire."

CHAPTER VIII.

THE FABLES.

IT was beyond a doubt his practice in translation, and the remarkable success that attended it, which suggested to Dryden the last, and one of the most singular, but at the same time the most brilliantly successful of all his poetical experiments. His translations themselves were in many cases rather paraphrases than translations. He now conceived the idea of a kind of composition which was to be avowedly paraphrase. With the unfailing catholicity of taste which is one of his finest literary characteristics, he had always avoided the ignorant contempt with which the age was wont to look on mediæval literature. Even Cowley, we are told, when requested by one of his patrons to give an opinion on Chaucer, confessed that he could not relish him. If, when he planned an Arthurian epic, Dryden had happened to hit on the idea of "transversing" Mallory, we might have had an additional star of the first magnitude in English literature, though his ability to produce a wholly original epic may be doubted. At sixty-seven, writing hard for subsistence, he could not think of any such mighty attempt as this. But he took certain tales of Chaucer, and certain novels of Chaucer's master, Boccaccio, and applied his system to them. The result was the book of poems to which, including as it did many Ovidian translations, and much other verse, he gave the name of *Fables*, using that word in its simple sense of stories. It is not surprising that this book took the town by storm. Enthusiastic critics, even at the beginning of the present century, assigned to *Theodore and Honoria* "a place on the very topmost shelf of English poetry." Such arrangements depend, of course, upon the definition of poetry itself. But I venture to think that it would be almost sufficient case against any such definition, that it should exclude the finest passages of the *Fables* from a position a little lower than that which Ellis assigned to them. It so happens that we are, at the present day, in a position to put Dryden to a specially crucial test which his contemporaries were unable to apply. To us Chaucer is no longer an ingenious and intelligent but illegible barbarian. We read the *Canterbury Tales* with as much relish, and with nearly as little difficulty, as we read Spenser, or Milton, or Pope, or Byron, or our own living poets. *Palamon and Arcite* has, therefore, to us the drawback—if drawback it be—of being confronted on equal terms with its original. Yet I venture to say that, except in the case of those unfortunate persons whose only way of showing appreciation of one thing is by depreciation of something else, an acquaintance with the *Knight's Tale* injures Dryden's work hardly at all. There could not possibly be a severer test of at least formal excellence than this.

The *Fables* were published in a folio volume which, according to the contract with Tonson, was to contain 10,000 verses. The payment was 300*l.*, of which 250 guineas were paid down at the time of agreement, when three-fourths of the stipulated number of lines were actually handed over to the publisher. On this occasion, at least, Jacob had not to complain of an unduly small consideration. For Dryden gave him not 2500, but nearly 5000 verses more, without, as far as is known, receiving any increase of his fee. The remainder of the 300*l.* was not to be paid till the appearance of a second edition, and this did not actually take place until some years after the poet's death. Pope's statement, therefore, that Dryden received "sixpence a line" for his verses, though not formally accurate, was sufficiently near the truth. It is odd that one of the happiest humours of Tom the First (Shadwell) occurring in a play written long before he quarrelled with Dryden, concerns this very practice of payment by line. In the *Sullen Lovers* one of the characters complains that his bookseller has refused him twelvepence a line, when the intrinsic worth of some verses is at least ten shillings, and all can be proved to be worth three shillings "to the veriest Jew in Christendom." So that Tonson was not alone in the adoption of the method. As the book finally appeared, the *Fables* contained, besides prefatory matter and dedications, five pieces from Chaucer (*Palamon and Arcite*, the *Cock and the Fox*, the *Flower and the Leaf*, the *Wife of Bath's Tale*, the *Character of a Good Parson*), three from Boccaccio (*Sigismonda and Guiscardo*, *Theodore and Honoria*, *Cymon and Iphigenia*), the first book of the *Iliad*, some versions of Ovid's *Metamorphoses* in continuation of others previously published, an *Epistle to John Driden*, the second *St. Cecilia Ode*, commonly called *Alexander's Feast*, and an *Epitaph*.

The book was dedicated to the Duke of Ormond in a prose epistle, than which even Dryden never did anything better. It abounds with the fanciful expressions, just stopping short of conceit, which were such favourites with him, and which

he managed perhaps better than any other writer. He holds
of the Ormond family, he tells the Duke, by a tenure of
dedications, having paid that compliment to his Grace's
grandfather, the great Duke of Ormond, and having
celebrated Ossory in memorial verses. Livy, Publicola,
and the history of Peru are brought in perhaps somewhat
by the head and shoulders ; but this was simply the
fashion of the time, and the manner of the doing fully
excused it. Even this piece, however, falls short, in point
of graceful flattery, of the verse dedication of *Palamon and
Arcite* to the Duchess. Between the two is the preface,
which contains a rather interesting history of the genesis
of the *Fables*. After doing the first book of Homer " as
an essay to the whole work," it struck Dryden that he
would try some of the passages on Homeric subjects in
the *Metamorphoses*, and these in their turn led to others.
When he had sufficiently extracted the sweets of Ovid,
" it came into my mind that our old English poet Chaucer
in many things resembled him ;" and then, " as thoughts,
according to Mr. Hobbs, have always some connexion,"
he was led to think of Boccaccio. The preface continues
with critical remarks upon all three authors and their
position in the history of their respective literatures, remarks which, despite some almost unavoidable ignorance
on the writer's part as to the early condition and mutual
relationship of modern languages, are still full of interest
and value. It ends a little harshly, but naturally enough,
in a polemic with Blackmore, Milbourn, and Collier.
Not much need be said about the causes of either of these
debates. Macaulay has told the Collier story well, and,
on the whole, fairly enough, though he is rather too complimentary to the literary value of Collier's work. That
redoubtable divine had all the right on his side, beyond a

doubt, but he sometimes carried his argument a good deal
too far.   Dryden, however, could not defend himself, and
he knew this, and did not attempt it, though he could
not always refrain, now and afterwards, from indulging in
little flings at Collier.   Blackmore had two causes of
quarrel with Dryden—one the same as Collier's, the other
a political one, the poetical knight being a staunch Whig.
Milbourn was an obscure country clergyman, who had at
one time been a great admirer of Dryden, as a letter of
his still extant, in which he orders the poet's works to be
sent to him, shows.   He had, however, fallen foul of
the *Virgil*, for which he received from Dryden due and
perhaps more than due castigation.

Enough has been already said of the translations of
Homer and Ovid.   The latter, however, are, as far as
mere verse goes, among the best of all the translations.
Palamon and Arcite, however, and all the other contents
of the book are of a very different order of interest.
Dryden had an extreme admiration for this story, which
as the subject for an epic he thought as good as either
Homer's or Virgil's.   Nowadays most people have left
off considering the technical value of different subjects,
which is no doubt a misfortune.   But it is easy to see
that the legend, with its interesting incidents, its contrast
of character, its revolutions, and so forth, does actually
come very near to the perfect idea of the artificial epic.
The comparative nullity of the heroine would have been
thought no drawback in ancient art.   Dryden has divided
the story into three books, and has, as usual, paraphrased
with the utmost freedom, but he has kept closer to the
dimensions of the original than is his wont.   His three
books do not much exceed the length of the original tale.
In the different parts, however, he has used his own dis-

cretion in amplifying or contracting exactly as he thinks
proper, and the comparison of different passages with the
original thus brings out in a manifold way the idiosyncra-
sies of the two writers. Perhaps this is nowhere more
marked than in the famous description of the Temple of
Mars. As far as the temple itself goes, Dryden has the
upper hand, but he is beaten when it comes to " the portraiture which was upon the wall." Sometimes he has
simply adopted Chaucer's very words, sometimes he has
done otherwise, and then he has almost always done
worse. The " smiler with the knife under the cloak " is
very inadequately replaced by three whole lines about
hypocrisy. If the couplet

> Amiddes of the temple sate Mischance,
> And Discomfort and sory Countenance,

be contrasted with

> In midst of all the dome Misfortune sate,
> And gloomy Discontent and fell Debate,

the comparatively otiose epithets which in the next century were to be the curse of the style, strike the eye and
ear very forcibly. Indeed, in this most finished work
of Dryden's nothing is easier than to see the strength and
the weakness of the method he had introduced. In his
hands it turns almost always to strength. But in thus
boldly bringing his work side by side with Chaucer's, he
had indicated the divergence which was to be carried
farther and farther by his followers, until the *mot propre*
was lost altogether in a washy sea of elegant epithets and
flowing versification. That time, however, was far off, or
might have seemed to be far off, to a reader of the
Fables. It is only when Chaucer is actually compared
that the defects, or rather the possibilities of defect, rise
to the eye. If *Palamon and Arcite* be read by itself, it is

almost entirely delightful, and, as has been said already,
it will even bear the strain of comparison. For the loss
is counterbalanced by gain, gain of sustained strength and
greater perfection of workmanship, even though we may
know well enough that Dryden's own idea of Chaucer's
shortcomings in versification was a mere delusion.

The *Nun's Priest's Tale* was also not very much extended, though it was considerably altered in Dryden's
version, entitled *The Cock and the Fox*. Dryden's fond-
ness for the beast-story had, as we have seen already,
drawn upon him the reprehension of Messrs. Prior and
Montague, critics of severe and cultivated taste. It has
just been suggested that a great loss has been sustained
by his not having taken the fancy to transverse some
Arthurian stories. In the same way, if he had known the
original *Roman de Renart*, he would doubtless have made
good use of it. *The Cock and the Fox* itself is inferior to
many of the branches of the old tree, but it has not a few
merits, and the story of the two friends is one of the very
best things of the kind. To this Dryden has done ample
justice. But in the original not the least attractive part
is the solemn profusion of learned names and citations
characteristic of the fourteenth century, which the translator has in some cases thought it better to omit. It may
not be quite clear whether Chaucer, who generally had a
kind of satirical undercurrent of intention in him, was
serious in putting these into the mouths of Partlet and
Chanticleer or not, but still one misses them. On the
other hand, Dryden has made the most of the astrological
allusions. For it must be remembered that he had a decided hankering after astrology, like many of the greatest
men of his century. Of this there is evidence quite apart
from Mrs. Thomas's stories, which also deal with the point.

The third of Dryden's Chaucerian versions is one of the
most charming of all, and this, though the variations from
the original are considerable, and though that original is
itself one of the most delightful works of the kind.[1]   I
have read, perhaps as much as most Englishmen, the
French fourteenth-century poetry on which so much of
Chaucer's is modelled, but I hardly know either in French
or English a poem more characteristic, and more delight-
fully characteristic of the fourteenth century than the
Flower and the Leaf. The delight in a certain amiable kind
of natural beauty, the transference of the signs and symbols
of that beauty to the service of a fantastic and yet not un-
natural poetry of love, the introduction of abstract and
supernatural beings to carry out sometimes by allegory
and sometimes by personification the object of the poet,
are all exemplified in this little piece of some 500 or 600
lines, in a manner which it would be hard to match in
Froissart or Guillaume de Machault. Yet Dryden has
asserted his power of equalling the virtue of the original
in what may be called an original translation.   The two
poems differ from one another considerably in details of
machinery and imagery.   Chaucer is happier in his descriptions of nature, Dryden in the representation of the
central personages.   But both alike have the power of
transporting.   Even now, when so much of his language
and machinery have become hackneyed, Dryden can
exert this power on those who are well acquainted with
mediæval literature, who have felt its strange fascination,
and the ease with which it carries off the reader into
unfamiliar and yet delightful lands, where nothing is dis-

---

[1] I do not here concern myself with the hypothesis of the
spuriousness of this poem.

turbing and unreasonable, and yet everything is surprising
and unhackneyed. How much more strongly this power
must have been exerted on a singularly prosaic age, in which
the majority of persons would, like Prior and Montague,
have cast aside as nonsense worthy only of children the
gracious shadowy imaginations of mediæval thought, we in
the nineteenth century can hardly put ourselves in the
condition to estimate. But it must always remain one of
Dryden's highest titles to fame that he was able thus to
make extremes meet. He seems indeed to have had not
only the far from ordinary faculty of recognizing good
literature wherever he met it, but the quite extraordinary
faculty of making other people recognize it too by translating it into the language which they were capable of
comprehending. A passage may be worth quoting :—

> To this the dame replied : " Fair daughter, know,
> That what you saw was all a fairy show ;
> And all those airy shapes you now behold
> Were human bodies once, and clothed with earthly mould.
> Our souls, not yet prepared for upper light,
> Till doomsday wander in the shades of night ;
> This only holiday of all the year,
> We, privileged, in sunshine may appear ;
> With songs and dance we celebrate the day,
> And with due honours usher in the May.
> At other times we reign by night alone,
> And posting through the skies pursue the moon ;
> But when the morn arises, none are found,
> For cruel Demogorgon walks the round,
> And if he finds a fairy lag in light,
> He drives the wretch before, and lashes into night.
>   " All courteous are by kind ; and ever proud
> With friendly offices to help the good.
> In every land we have a larger space
> Than what is known to you of mortal race ;
> Where we with green adorn our fairy bowers,
> And even this grove, unseen before, is ours.

Know farther, every lady clothed in white,
And crowned with oak and laurel every knight,
Are servants to the Leaf, by liveries known
Of innocence ; and I myself am one.
Saw you not her so graceful to behold,
In white attire, and crowned with radiant gold ?
The sovereign lady of our land is she,
Diana called, the queen of chastity ;
And, for the spotless name of maid she bears,
That *Agnus castus* in her hand appears ;
And all her train, with leafy chaplets crowned,
Were for unblamed virginity renowned ;
But those the chief and highest in command
Who bear those holy branches in their hand,
The knights adorned with laurel crowns are they,
Whom death nor danger ever could dismay,
Victorious names, who made the world obey :
Who, while they lived, in deeds of arms excelled,
And after death for deities were held.
But those who wear the woodbine on their brow,
Were knights of love, who never broke their vow ;
Firm to their plighted faith, and ever free
From fears, and fickle chance, and jealousy.
The lords and ladies, who the woodbine bear,
As true as Tristram and Isotta were."

Why Dryden selected the *Wife of Bath's Tale* among his
few translations from Chaucer, it is not very easy to say.
It is a sufficiently harmless *fabliau*, but it cannot be said
to come up in point of merit to many others of the *Canterbury Tales*. The enemies of our poet would doubtless
say that he selected it because of the unfavourable opinions
as to womankind which it contains. But then those
same enemies would find it difficult to say why he did not
choose instead the scandalous prologue which unites
opinions of womankind at least as unfavourable with
other matter of the sort which hostile criticism supposes
to have been peculiarly tempting to Dryden. In the

actual tale as given in the *Fables* there is some alloy of this kind, but nothing that could be at all shocking to the age. The length of the story is in proportion more amplified than is the case with the others. Probably the argumentative gifts of the old hag who turned out not to be an old hag attracted Dryden, for he was always at his best, and must have known that he was always at his best, in passages of the kind. The pleading of the crone is one of his best efforts. A certain desultoriness which is to be found in Chaucer is changed into Dryden's usual chain of serried argument, and it is much less surprising in the translation than in the original that the knight should have decided to submit at once to such a she-lawyer. But the " wife " herself has something to complain of Dryden. Her fancy for widowhood is delicately enough put in the original :—

> [Sende] grace to overlive them that we wed.

Dryden makes it much blunter :—

> May widows wed as often as they can,
> And ever for the better change their man.

The Character of a Good Parson admits itself to be "enlarged" from Chaucer, and indeed the termination, to the extent of some forty lines, is wholly new, and written with special reference to the circumstances of the time. To this character there is a pleasant little story attached. It seems from a letter to Pepys that the diarist had himself recommended the character in the original to Dryden's notice. When the verses were done, the poet told Pepys of the fact, and proposed to bring them for his inspection. The answer contained a sentence which displays a much greater antipathy to parsons than that which, if we may believe Lord Macaulay, who perhaps borrowed the idea from Stillingfleet or Collier, Dryden himself felt. Pepys remarks that he hopes "from your copy of this good parson to fancy some amends made me for the hourly offence I bear with from the sight of so many lewd originals." What particular trouble Pepys had to bear at the hands of the lewd originals it would be hard to say. But—time-server as he had once been—he was in all probability sufficiently Jacobite at heart to relish the postscript in Dryden's version. This transfers the circumstances of the expulsion of the Nonjurors to the days of Richard the Second and Henry of Bolingbroke. Nor, had there still been a censorship of the press, is it at all probable that this postscript would have been passed for publication. The following verses are sufficiently pointed :—

> Conquest, an odious name, was laid aside ;
> When all submitted, none the battle tried.
> The senseless plea of right by providence
> Was by a flattering priest invented since,
> And lasts no longer than the present sway,
> But justifies the next which comes in play.
> The people's right remains ; let those who dare
> Dispute their power when they the judges are.

The character itself is also very much enlarged ; so much so, that the original can only be said to have furnished the heads for it. Dryden has done few better things.

The selections from Boccaccio, like those from Chaucer, may or may not have been haphazard. The first, at any rate, which has been as a rule the worst thought of, explains itself sufficiently. The story of *Tancred and Sigismunda* perhaps afforded room for " loose descriptions : " it certainly afforded room for the argument in verse of which Dryden was so great a master. Although the hints of the original have been somewhat coarsely

amplified, the speech of Sigismunda is still a very noble
piece of verse, and her final address to her husband's
heart almost better.   Here is a specimen :—

> " Thy praise (and thine was then the public voice)
> First recommended Guiscard to my choice :
> Directed thus by thee, I looked, and found
> A man I thought deserving to be crowned ;
> First by my father pointed to my sight,
> Nor less conspicuous by his native light ;
> His mind, his mien, the features of his face,
> Excelling all the rest of human race :
> These were thy thoughts, and thou couldst judge aright,
> Till interest made a jaundice in thy sight.
> Or should I grant thou didst not rightly see,
> Then thou wert first deceived, and I deceived by thee.
> But if thou shalt allege, through pride of mind,
> Thy blood with one of base condition joined,
> 'Tis false ; for 'tis not baseness to be poor :
> His poverty augments thy crime the more ;
> Upbraids thy justice with the scant regard
> Of worth ; whom princes praise, they should reward
> Are these the kings intrusted by the crowd
> With wealth, to be dispensed for common good ?
> The people sweat not for their king's delight,
> To enrich a pimp, or raise a parasite ;
> Theirs is the toil ; and he who well has served
> His country, has his country's wealth deserved.
> Even mighty monarchs oft are meanly born,
> And kings by birth to lowest rank return ;
> All subject to the power of giddy chance,
> For fortune can depress, or can advance ;
> But true nobility is of the mind,
> Not given by chance, and not to chance resigned.
> " For the remaining doubt of thy decree,
> What to resolve, and how dispose of me ;
> Be warned to cast that useless care aside,
> Myself alone will for myself provide.
> If in thy doting and decrepit age,
> Thy soul, a stranger in thy youth to rage,

Begins in cruel deeds to take delight,
Gorge with my blood thy barbarous appetite;
For I so little am disposed to pray
For life, I would not cast a wish away.
Such as it is, the offence is all my own;
And what to Guiscard is already done,
Or to be done, is doomed by thy decree,
That, if not executed first by thee,
Shall on my person be performed by me.
  "Away! with women weep, and leave me here,
Fixed, like a man, to die without a tear;
Or save, or slay us both this present hour,
'Tis all that fate has left within thy power."

The last of the three, *Cymon and Iphigenia*, has been a
great favourite. In the original it is one of the most un-
interesting stories of the *Decameron*, the single incident
of Cymon's falling in love, of which not very much is
made, being the only relief to a commonplace tale of
violence and treachery, in which neither the motives nor
the characters of the actors sufficiently justify them. The
Italian too, by making Iphigenia an unwilling captive,
takes away from Cymon the only excuse he could have
had. The three charming lines with which Dryden's
poem opens,

Old as I am, for lady's love unfit,
The power of beauty I remember yet,
Which once inflamed my soul, and still inspires my wit,

have probably bribed a good many readers, and certainly
the whole volume of the *Fables* is an ample justification of the poet's boast, not only as regards beauty of one
kind, but of all. The opening triplet is followed by a
diatribe against Collier, which at first seems in very bad
taste; but it is made with excellent art to lead on to a
description of the power of love, to which the story yokes

itself most naturally. Nor is any praise too high for the description of the actual scene in which Cymon is converted
from his brutishness by the sight of Iphigenia, an incident
of which, as has been said, the original takes small account.
But even with the important alterations which Dryden
has introduced into it, the story, as a story, remains of but
second-rate interest.

Nothing of this sort can be said of *Theodore and
Honoria*. I have said that Ellis's commendation of it may
be excessive. But that it goes at the head of all the poetry
of the school of which Dryden was a master is absolutely
certain. The original here is admirably suggestive : the
adaptation is more admirable in its obedience to the suggestions. It has been repeatedly noticed with what art
Dryden has gradually led up to the horror of the phantom
lady's appearance, which is in the original introduced in
an abrupt and casual way ; while the matter-of-factness of
the spectre's address, both to Theodore himself and to
the friends who wish afterwards to interfere in his
victim's favour, is most happily changed in the English
poem. Boccaccio indeed, master as he was of a certain
kind of pathos, did not, at least in the *Decameron*, succeed
with this particular sort of tragedy. His narrative has
altogether too much of the chronicle in it to be fully im-
pressive. Here Dryden's process of amplification has
been of the utmost service. At almost every step of the
story he has introduced new touches which transform it
altogether, and leave it at the close a perfect piece of narrative of the horrible kind. The same abruptness which
has been noticed in the original version of the earlier part
of the story appears in the later. In Dryden, Honoria,
impressed with the sight and with Theodore's subsequent
neglect of her, dreams of what she has seen, and thinks

over what she has dreamt, at last, and only at last, resolving to subdue her pride and consent to Theodore's suit.
Boccaccio's heroine goes straight home in a business-like
manner, and sends "a trusty damsel" that very evening
to inform her lover that she surrenders. This is, to say
the least, sudden. In short, the comparison is here
wholly in favour of the English poet. Nor if we drop
the parallel, and look at *Theodore and Honoria* merely
by itself, is it less admirable.

The purely original poems remain to be noticed. Of
the *Epistle to John Driden* we know that Dryden himself thought highly, while the person to whom it was
addressed was so pleased with it that he gave him "a
noble present," said by family tradition to have been
500*l.*, but which Malone, *ex sua conjectura*, reduces to
100*l.* John Driden was the poet's cousin, and his
frequent host at Chesterton. He was a bachelor, his
house being kept by his sister Honor ; he was a member
of Parliament and an enthusiastic sportsman. Chesterton
had come into the Dryden family by marriage, and John
Driden inherited it as the second son. The poem contains, in allusion to Driden's bachelorhood, one of those
objurgations on matrimony which have been interpreted in
a personal sense, but which are, in all probability, merely
the commonplaces of the time. Besides wives, physicians were a frequent subject of Dryden's satire ; and
the passage in this poem about the origin of medicine has
been learnt by almost every one. It might not have been
written but for Blackmore's sins, for Dryden had, in the
postscript to his *Virgil*, paid an elaborate compliment to two
ornaments of the profession. But it is naturally enough
connected with a compliment to his cousin's sportsman-
ship. Then there is what might be called a "Character of

a good Member of Parliament," fashioned, of course, to suit the case of the person addressed, who, though not exactly a Jacobite, was a member of the Opposition. The poem ends with a most adroit compliment at once to the subject and to the writer. These complimentary pieces always please posterity with a certain drawback, unless, like the lines to Congreve, and the almost more beautiful lines on Oldham, they deal with merits which are still in evidence, and are not merely personal. But the judgment of Dorset and Montague, who thought of this piece and of the exquisite verses to the Duchess of Ormond that he "never writ better," was not far wrong.

The only piece that remains to be noticed is better known even than the *Epistle to John Driden*. *Alexander's Feast* was the second ode which Dryden wrote for the "Festival of St. Cecilia." He received for it 40*l*., which, as he tells his sons that the writing of it "would be noways beneficial," was probably unexpected, if the statement as to the payment is true. There are other legendary contradictions about the time occupied in writing it, one story saying that it was done in a single night, while another asserts that he was a fortnight in composing or correcting it. But, as has been frequently pointed out, the two statements are by no means incompatible. Another piece of gossip about this famous ode is that Dryden at first wrote Lais instead of Thais, which "small mistake" he bids Tonson in a letter to remember to alter. Little criticism of *Alexander's Feast* is necessary. Whatever drawbacks its form may have (especially the irritating chorus), it must be admitted to be about the best thing of its kind, and nothing more can be demanded of any poetry than to be excellent in its kind. Dryden himself

thought it the best of all his poetry, and he had a remarkable faculty of self-criticism.

This volume of poems was not only the last that Dryden
produced, but it also exhibits his poetical character in its
very best and most perfect form.   He had, through all his
long literary life, been constantly a student, always his own
scholar, always correcting, varying, re-arranging, and re-
fining.   The citations already given will have shown
at what perfection of metre he had by this time arrived.
Good as his early (if not his earliest) works are in this
respect, it must be remembered that it was long before he
attained his greatest skill.   Play-writing in rhyme and
blank verse, practice in stanzas, and pindarics, and irregular
lyrical measures, all went to furnish him with the experience he required, and which certainly was not in his
case the school of a fool.

Beginning with a state of pupilage to masters who were
none of the best, he subsequently took little instruction,
except of a fragmentary kind, from any living man except
Milton in poetry, and, as he told Congreve, Tillotson in prose.
But he was none the less constantly teaching himself.   His
vocabulary is naturally a point of great importance in any
consideration of his influence on our literature.   His earliest
work exhibits many traces of the scholastic and pedantic
phraseology of his immediate forerunners.   It is probable
that in his second period, when his activity was chiefly
dramatic, he might have got rid of this, had not the tendency been strengthened by the influence of Milton.   At
one period, again, the Gallicizing tendencies of the time
led him to a very improper and inexcusable importation
of French words.   This, however, he soon dropped.   In
the meridian of his powers, when his great satires were
produced, these tendencies, the classical and the Gallican,

in action and re-action with his full command of English,
vernacular and literary, produced a dialect which, if not the
most graceful that the language has ever known, is perhaps the strongest and most nervous.   Little change takes
place in the last twenty years, though the tendency to
classicism and archaism, strengthened it may be by the work
of translation, not unfrequently reappears.   In versification the great achievement of Dryden was the alteration
of what may be called the balance of the line, causing it to
run more quickly and to strike its rhymes with a sharper
and less prolonged sound.   One obvious means of obtain-
ing this end was, as a matter of course, the isolation of
the couplet and the avoidance of overlapping the different lines one upon the other.   The effect of this overlapping, by depriving the eye and voice of the expectation
of rest at the end of each couplet, is always one of two
things.   Either the lines are converted into a sort of
rhythmic prose, made musical by the rhymes rather than
divided by them, or else a considerable pause is invited at
the end of each, or of most lines, and the cadence of the
whole becomes comparatively slow and languid.   Both
these forms, as may be seen in the works of Mr. Morris,
as well as in the older writers, are excellently suited for
narration of some considerable length.   They are less well
suited for satire, for argument, and for the moral reflections
which the age of Dryden loved.   He therefore set himself
to elaborate the couplet with its sharp point, its quick
delivery, and the pistol-like detonation of its rhyme.   But
there is an obvious objection, or rather there are several
obvious objections which present themselves to the couplet.
It was natural that to one accustomed to the more varied
range of the older rhythm and metre, there might seem
to be a danger of the snip-snap monotony into which, as

we know, it did actually fall when it passed out of the
hands of its first great practitioners.   There might also be
a fear that it would not always be possible to compress
the sense of a complete clause within the narrow limits of
twenty syllables.   To meet these difficulties Dryden re-
sorted to three mechanical devices,—the hemistich, the
Alexandrine, and the triplet; all three of which could be
used indifferently to eke out the space or to give variety
of sound.   The use of the hemistich, or fragmentary line,
appears to have been based partly on the well-known practice of Virgil, partly on the necessities of dramatic composition where the unbroken English couplet is to English
ears intolerable.   In poetry proper the hemistich is anything but pleasing, and Dryden becoming convinced of
the fact almost discarded it.   The Alexandrine and the
triplet he always continued to use, and they are to this
day the most obvious characteristics, to a casual observer,
of his versification.   To the Alexandrine, judiciously used,
and limited to its proper acceptation of a verse of twelve
syllables, I can see no objection.   The metre, though a well-
known English critic has maltreated it of late, is a very
fine one; and some of Dryden's own lines are unmatched examples of that " energy divine " which has been attributed
to him.   In an essay on the Alexandrine in English poetry,
which yet remains to be written, and which would be not
the least valuable of contributions to poetical criticism,
this use of the verse would have to be considered, as well
as its regular recurrent employment at the close of the
Spenserian stanza, and its continuous use, of which not
many poets besides Drayton and Mr. Browning have given
us considerable examples.   An examination of the *Poly-
olbion* and of *Fifine at the Fair*, side by side, would, I think,
reveal capacities somewhat unexpected even in this form

of arrangement. But so far as the occasional Alexandrine is concerned, it is not a hyperbole to say that a number, out of all proportion, of the best lines in English poetry may be found in the closing verses of the Spenserian stave as used by Spenser himself, by Shelley, and by the present Laureate, and in the occasional Alexandrines of Dryden. The only thing to be said against this latter use is, that it demands a very skilful ear and hand to adjust the cadence. So much for the Alexandrine.

For the triplet I must confess myself to be entirely without affection. Except in the very rare cases when its contents come in, in point of sense, as a kind of parenthesis or aside, it seems to me to spoil the metre, if anything could spoil Dryden's verse. That there was some doubt about it even in the minds of those who used it, may be inferred from the care they generally took to accompany it in print with the bracket indicator, as if to invite the eye to break it gently to the ear. So strong was Dryden's verse, so well able to subdue all forms to its own measure, that in him it mattered but little ; in his followers its drawbacks at once appeared.

A few personal details not already alluded to remain as to Dryden's life at this time. To this period belongs the second and only other considerable series of his letters. They are addressed to Mrs. Steward, a cousin of his, though of a much younger generation. Mrs. Steward was the daughter of Mrs. Creed, the already-mentioned indefatigable decorator of Northamptonshire churches and halls, and she herself was given to the arts of painting and poetry. She had married Mr. Elmes Steward, a mighty sportsman, whose house at Cotterstock still exists by the roadside from Oundle to Peterborough. The correspondence extends over the last eighteen months of the

poet's life, beginning in October, 1698, and not ending till
a week or two before his death in the spring of 1700.
Mrs. Steward is said to have been about eight-and-twenty
at the time, and beautiful. The first letter speaks of a visit
soon to be paid to Cotterstock after many invitations,
and is rather formal in style. Thenceforward, however,
the epistles, sometimes addressed to Mr. Steward (Dryden
not infrequently spells it Stewart and Stuart), and sometimes to his wife, are very cordial, and full of thanks for
presents of country produce. On one occasion Dryden
"intends" that Lady Elizabeth should "taste the plover
he had received," an incident upon which, if I were a
commentator, I should build a legend of conjugal happi-
ness quite as plausible, and probably quite as well founded,
as the legend of conjugal unhappiness which has actually
been constructed. Then there are injurious allusions to a
certain parson's wife at Tichmarsh, who is "just the contrary" of Mrs. Steward. Marrow puddings are next
acknowledged, which it seems were so good that they had
quite spoiled Charles Dryden's taste for any other. Then
comes that sentence, "Old men are not so insensible of
beauty as, it may be, you young ladies think," which was
elsewhere translated into eloquent verse, and the same
letter describes the writer as passing his time " sometimes
with Ovid, sometimes with our old English poet Chaucer."
More acknowledgments of presents follow, and then a
visit is promised, with the prayer that Mrs. Steward will
have some small beer brewed for him without hops, or with
a very inconsiderable quantity, because the bitter beer at
Tichmarsh had made him very ill. The visit came off in
August, 1699, and it is to be hoped that the beer was not
bitter. After his return the poet sends, in the pleasant
old fashion, a history of his journey back to London,

whither the stage coach took him out of his way, whereby
not passing certain friends' houses, he missed " two couple
of rabbits, and Mr. Cole's Ribadavia wine," a stirrup cup
of the latter being probably intended.　In November occurs the famous description of himself as " a man who has
done his best to improve the language, and especially the
poetry," with much literary and political gossip, and
occasional complaints of bad health.　This letter may.
perhaps be quoted as a specimen :—

Nov. 7, 1699.

MADAM,—Even your expostulations are pleasing to me ; for
though they show you angry, yet they are not without many
expressions of your kindness ; and therefore I am proud to be
so chidden.　Yet I cannot so farr abandon my own defence, as to
confess any idleness or forgetfulness on my part.　What has
hind'red me from writeing to you, was neither ill health, nor, a
worse thing, ingratitude ; but a flood of little businesses, which
yet are necessary to my subsistance, and of which I hop'd to
have given you a good account before this time : but the Court
rather speaks kindly of me, than does anything for me, though
they promise largely ; and perhaps they think I will advance as
they go backward, in which they will be much deceiv'd ; for I
can never go an inch beyond my conscience and my honour.　If
they will consider me as a man who has done my best to improve the language, and especially the poetry, and will be content with my acquiescence under the present government, and
forbearing satire on it, that I can promise, because I can perform
it ; but I can neither take the oaths, nor forsake my religion ;
because I know not what church to go to, if I leave the Catho-
lique ; they are all so divided amongst themselves in matters of
faith necessary to salvation, and yet all assumeing the name of
Protestants.　May God be pleased to open your eyes, as he has
open'd mine !　Truth is but one ; and they who have once
heard of it, can plead no excuse, if they do not embrace it.　But
these are things too serious for a trifling letter.　If you desire
to hear anything more of my affairs, the Earl of Dorsett, and

your cousin Montague, have both seen the two poems, to the Duchess of Ormond and my worthy cousin Driden; and are of opinion, that I never writt better. My other friends are divided in their judgments, which to preferr; but the greater part are for those to my dear kinsman; which I have corrected with so much care, that they will now be worthy of his sight, and do neither of us any dishonour after our death.

There is this day to be acted a new tragedy, made by Mr. Hopkins, and, as I believe, in rhime. He has formerly written a play in verse, called *Boadicea*, which you fair ladyes lik'd; and is a poet who writes good verses, without knowing how or why; I mean, he writes naturally well, without art, or learning, or good sence. Congreve is ill of the gout at Barnet Wells. I have had the honour of a visite from the Earl of Dorsett, and din'd with him. Matters in Scotland are in a high ferment, and next door to a breach betwixt the two nations; but they say from court, that France and we are hand and glove. 'Tis thought the king will endeavour to keep up a standing army, and make the stirr in Scotland his pretence for it; my cousin Driden, and the country party, I suppose, will be against it; for when a spirit is raised, 'tis hard conjuring him down again. You see I am dull by my writeing news; but it may be my cousin Creed may be glad to hear what I believe is true, though not very pleasing. I hope he recovers health in the country, by his staying so long in it. My service to my cousin Stuart, and all at Oundle.

I am, faire Cousine,

Your most obedient servant,

JOHN DRYDEN.

For Mrs. Stewart, Att
    Cotterstock, near Oundle,
        In Northamptonshire,
            These.
      To be left at the Post-house in Oundle.

CHAPTER IX.

DRYDEN's life lasted but a very short time after the publication of the *Fables*. He was, if not a very old man, close upon his seventieth year. He had worked hard, and had probably lived no more carefully than most of the men of his time. Gout, gravel, and other disorders tormented him sorely. The *Fables* were published in November, 1699, and during the winter he was more or less ill. As has been mentioned, many letters of his exist in reference to this time, more in proportion than for any other period of his life. Besides those to Mrs. Steward, there are some addressed to Mrs. Thomas, a young and pretty literary lady, who afterwards fell among the Philistines, and who made use of her brief intimacy with the Dryden family to romance freely about it, when in her later days she was indigent, in prison, and what was worse, in the employ of Curll. One of these letters contains the frankest and most graceful of Dryden's many apologies for the looseness of his writings, accompanied by a caution to " Corinna " against following the example of the illustrious Aphra Behn, a caution which was a good deal needed, though unfortunately fruitless. In the early spring of 1700, or, according to the calendar of the day, in the last months of 1699, some of Dryden's admirers got up a

N

benefit performance for him at the Duke's Theatre.
Fletcher's *Pilgrim* was selected for the occasion, revised
by Vanbrugh, and with the addition of a lyrical scene by
Dryden himself. He also wrote for the occasion a secular
masque to celebrate the opening of the new century : the
controversy on the point whether 1700 belonged to the
seventeenth century or the eighteenth not having, it seems,
arisen. The performance took place, but the date of it is
uncertain, and it has been thought that it was not till
after Dryden's death. This happened in the following
wise. During the months of March and April Dryden
was very ill with gout. One toe became much inflamed,
and not being properly attended to, it mortified. Hobbs,
the surgeon, was then called in, and advised amputation,
but Dryden refused on the score of his age, and the
inutility of prolonging a maimed existence. The mortifi-
cation spreading further, it was a case for amputation of
the entire leg, with probably dubious results, or else for
certain death. On the 30th of April the *Postboy* announced that "John Dryden, Esq., the famous poet, lies
a-dying," and at three o'clock the next morning he died
very quietly and peacefully.

His funeral was sufficiently splendid. Halifax is said
to have at first offered to discharge the whole cost himself,
but other friends were anxious to share it, among whom
Dorset and Lord Jeffreys, the Chancellor's son, are specially mentioned. The body was embalmed, and lay in
state at the College of Physicians for some days. On the
13th of May the actual funeral took place at Westminster
Abbey, with a great procession, preceded at the College by
a Latin oration from Garth the President, and by the
singing of *Exegi Monumentum* to music. Years afterwards
"Corinna" forged for Curll a wild account of the matter,

of which it is sufficient to say that it lacks the slightest
corroboration, and is intrinsically improbable, if not impossible. It may be found in most of the biographies,
and Malone has devoted his usual patient industry to its
demolition. Sometime passed before any monument was
erected to Dryden in Poet's Corner, where he had been
buried by Chaucer and Cowley. Pepys tells us that
Dorset and Montague were going to do it. But they did
not. Sometime later Congreve complimented the Duke
of Newcastle on having given order for a monument, a
compliment which his Grace obtained at a remarkably
cheap rate, for the order, if given, was never executed.
Finally, twenty years after his death, the Duke of Buck-
inghamshire, better known under his former title of Lord
Mulgrave, came to the rescue, it is said, owing to a reflection of Pope's on Dryden's " rude and nameless stone."
The monument was not magnificent, but at any rate it
saves the poet from such dishonour as there may be in a
nameless grave. The hymn sung at his funeral probably
puts that matter most sensibly.

Dryden's wife lived until 1714, and died a very old
woman and insane. Her children, like her husband, had
died before her. Charles, the eldest, was drowned in the
Thames near Datchet in 1704 ; John, the second, hardly
outlived his father a year, and died at Rome in 1701 ;
the third, Erasmus Henry, succeeded in 1710 to the
family honours, but died in the same year. The house of
Canons Ashby is still held by descendants of the family,
but in the female line; though the name has been unbroken,
and the title has been continued.

Something has already been said about the character of
Lady Elizabeth Dryden. It has to be added here that
the stories about her temper and relations with her hus-

band and his friends, bear investigation as little as those
about her maidenly conduct. Most of them are mere
hearsays, and some not even that. Dryden, it is said,
must have lived unhappily with his wife, for he is always
sneering at matrimony. It is sufficient to say that much
the same might be said of every writer (at least for the
stage) between the Restoration and the accession of Anne.
Even the famous line in *Absalom and Achitophel*, which
has caused such scandal, is a commonplace as old at least
as Jean de Meung and the *Roman de la Rose*. When
Malone, on the authority of a Lady Dryden who lived a
hundred years later, but without a tittle of documentary
evidence, tells us that Lady Elizabeth was a shrew, we really
must ask what is the value of such testimony? There is
one circumstantial legend which has been much relied on.
Dryden, it is said, was at work one day in his study, when
his wife came in, and could not make him listen to something she had to say. Thereupon said she in a pet, " I
wish I were a book, and then perhaps you would pay me
some attention." " Then, my dear," replied this graceless
bard, " pray be an almanac, that I may change you at the
end of the year." The joke cannot be said to be brilliant,
but, taking it as a true story, the notion of founding a
charge of conjugal unhappiness thereon is sufficiently
absurd. Mrs. Thomas's romancings are worthy of no
credit, and even if they were worthy of any, do not bear
much upon the question. All that can be said is, that the
few allusions to Lady Elizabeth in the poet's letters are
made in all propriety, and tell no tale of disunion. Of his
children it is allowed that he was excessively fond, and
his personal amiability is testified to with one consent by
all his friends who have left testimonies on the subject.
Congreve and " Granville the Polite " both mention his

modest and unassuming demeanour, and the obligingness
of his disposition. Pope, it is true, has brought against
him the terrible accusation that he was "not a genteel
man," being "intimate with none but poetical men."
The fact on which the charge seems to be based is more
than dubious, and Pope was evidently transferring his own
conception of Grub Street to the times when to be a
poetical man certainly was no argument against gentility.
Rochester, Mulgrave, Dorset, Sedley, Etherege, Roscommon,
make a very odd assortment of ungenteel poetical friends.

It is astonishing, when one comes to examine the
matter, how vague and shadowy our personal knowledge
of Dryden is. A handful of anecdotes, many of them
undated and unauthenticated except at third and fourth
hand, furnish us with almost all that we do know. That
he was fond of fishing, and prided himself upon being a
better fisherman than Durfey ; that he took a good deal of
snuff ; and that he did not drink much until Addison, in
the last years of his life, induced him to do so, almost
exhausts the lists of such traits which are recorded by
others. His " down look," his plumpness, his fresh colour
are points in which tradition is pretty well supported by
the portraits which exist, and by such evidence as can be
extracted from the libels against him. The famous picture
of him at Will's, which every one repeats, and which
Scott has made classical in the *Pirate*, is very likely true
enough to fact, and there is no harm in thinking of
Dryden in the great coffee-house, with his chair in
the balcony in summer, by the fire in winter, passing
criticisms and paying good-natured compliments on
matters literary. He had, he tells Mrs. Steward, a very
vulgar stomach—thus partially justifying Pope's accusations—and liked a chine of bacon better than marrow

puddings. He dignified Samuel Pepys with the title of *Padron Mio*, and was invited by Samuel to eat a cold chicken and a salad with him in return. According to one of the aimless gossiping stories, which are almost all we possess, he once stayed with Mulgrave at the great Yorkshire domain whence the title was derived, and was cheated by Mulgrave at bowls—a story not so unbelievable as Mr. Bell seems to think, for everybody cheated at play in those days ; and Mulgrave's disinclination to pay his trades-men, or in any other way to get rid of money, was notorious. But even the gossip which has come down to us is almost entirely literary. Thus we are told that when he allowed certain merits to " starch Johnny Crowne "—so called because of the unalterable stiffness and propriety of his collar and cravat—he used to add that " his father and Crowne's mother had been great friends." It is only fair to the reputation of Erasmus Dryden and of Mrs. Crowne to add that this must have been pure mischief, inasmuch as it is always said that the author of *Sir Courtly Nice* was born in Nova Scotia. His well-feigned denunciation of Smith and Johnson, his tormentors, or rather the tor-mentors of his Eidolon Bayes, as " the coolest and most insignificant fellows " he had ever seen on the stage, may be also recalled. Again, there is a legend that Bolingbroke, when a young man, came in one morning to see him, and found that he had been sitting up all night writing the ode on St. Cecilia's Day. Another time Bolingbroke called on him, and was asked to outstay Jacob Tonson, so as to prevent some apprehended incivility from the truculent Jacob. The story of his vexation at the liberty taken with him by Prior and Montague has been already mentioned more than once, but may be regarded with very considerable suspicion. Most famous perhaps of all

such legends is that which tells of the unlucky speech,
" Cousin Swift, you will never be a poet," than which
never was there anything more true or more unfortunate. Yet the enmity which, though it has been exaggerated, the greatest English man of letters in the next
generation felt towards his kinsman ought not to be
wholly regretted, because it has produced one of the most
touching instances of literal devotion which even a commentator ever paid to his idol. Swift, it must be remembered, has injuriously stigmatized Dryden's prefaces as being

> Merely writ at first for filling,
> To raise the volume's price a shilling.

Hereupon Malone has set to, and has gravely demon-
strated that, as the price at which plays were then issued
was fixed and constant, the insertion of a long preface
instead of a short one, or indeed of any preface at all,
could not have raised the volume's price a penny. Next
to Shadwell's criticism on *Macflecknoe*, I think this may
be allowed to be the happiest example recorded in connexion with the life of Dryden of the spirit of literalism.

Such idle stuff as these legends mostly are is indeed hardly
worth discussion, hardly even worth mentioning. The
quiet scenery of the Nene Valley, in which Dryden passed
all the beginning and not a little of the close of his life ;
the park at Charlton ; the river (an imaginary association
perhaps, but too striking a one to be lost) on which
Crites and Eugenius and Neander rowed down past
the " great roar of waters " at London Bridge, and
heard the Dutch guns as they talked of dramatic poesy ;
the house in Gerrard Street ; the balcony and coffee-room
at Will's ; the park where the king walked with the poet ;
and, last of all, the Abbey : these are the only scenes in
which Dryden can be pictured even by the most imagi-

native lover of the concrete picturesque. Very few days of his life of nearly seventy years emerge for us from the mass by virtue of any definite and detailed incident, the account of which we have on trustworthy authority. It is a commonplace to say that an author's life is in his works. But in Dryden's case it is a simple fact, and therefore a biography of him, let it be repeated at the close as it was asserted at the beginning, must consist of little but a discussion and running comment on those works, and on the characteristics, literary and personal, which are discoverable in them.

It only now remains to sum up these characteristics, which it must never be forgotten are of even more value because of the representative character of Dryden than because of his individual eminence. Many as are the great men of letters who have illustrated English literature from the beginning to the present day, it may safely be said that no one so represented his time and so influenced it as the man of letters whom we have been discussing. There are greater names in our literature, no doubt; there are others as great or nearly so. But at no time that I can think of was there any Englishman who, for a considerable period, was so far in advance of his contemporaries in almost every branch of literary work as Dryden was during the last twenty years of the seventeenth century. To turn a satiric couplet of his own, by the alteration of a single word, from an insult to a compliment, we may say that he, at any rate during his last decade,

> In prose and verse was owned without dispute
> Within the realms of *English* absolute.

But his representative character in relation to the men of his time was almost more remarkable than his intellectual and artistic superiority to them. Other great men of letters, with perhaps the single exception of Voltaire, have usually, when they represented their time at all, represented but a small part of it. With Dryden this was not the case. Not only did the immense majority of men of letters in his later days directly imitate him, but both then and earlier most literary Englishmen, even when they did not imitate him, worked on the same lines and pursued the same objects. The eighteen volumes of his works contain a faithful representation of the whole literary movement in England for the best part of half a century, and what is more, they contain the germs and indicate the direction of almost the whole literary movement for nearly a century more.

But Dryden was not only in his literary work a typical Englishman of his time, and a favourably typical one; he was almost as representative in point of character. The time was not the most showy or attractive in the moral history of the nation, though perhaps it looks to us not a little worse than it was. But it must be admitted to have been a time of shameless coarseness in language and manners; of virulent and bloodthirsty party-spirit; of almost unparalleled self-seeking and political dishonesty; and of a flattering servility to which, in the same way, hardly any parallel can be found. Its chief redeeming features were, that it was not a cowardly age, and, for the most part, not a hypocritical one. Men seem frequently to have had few convictions, and sometimes to have changed them with a somewhat startling rapidity. But when they had them, they had also the courage of them. They hit out with a vigour and a will which to this day is refreshing to read of; and when, as sometimes happened, they lost the battle, they took their punishment, as with perhaps some arrogance we are wont to say, like Englishmen. Dryden had the merits and the defects

eminently ; but the defects were, after all, in a mild and
by no means virulent form. His character has had exceedingly hard measure since. During the last ten years
of his life, and for the most part of the half-century suc-
cceding his death, his political principles were out of
favour, and this naturally prejudiced many persons against
his conduct even at the time when his literary eminence
was least questioned. In Johnson and in Scott, Dryden
found a brace of the doughtiest champions, as heartily
prepossessed in his favour as they were admirably armed
to fight his battles. But of late years he has again fallen
among the Philistines. It was obviously Lord Macaulay's
game to blacken the greatest literary champion of the
cause he had set himself to attack ; and I need not say
with what zest and energy Macaulay was wont to wield
the tar-brush. Some years later Dryden had the good
fortune to meet with an admirable editor of his poems.
I venture to think the late Mr. Christie's Globe edition
of our poet one of the very best things of the kind that
has ever been produced. From the purely literary point
of view there is scarcely a fault to be found with it. But
the editor unfortunately seems to have sworn allegiance
to Shaftesbury before he swore allegiance to Dryden.
He reconciled these jarring fealties by sacrificing the
character of the latter, while admitting his intellectual
greatness. An article to which I have more than once
referred in the *Quarterly Review* puts the facts once more
in a clear and fair light. But Mr. Green's twice-published
history has followed in the old direction, and has indeed
out-Macaulayed Macaulay in reckless abuse. I believe
that I have put the facts at least so that any reader who
takes the trouble may judge for himself of the private
conduct of Dryden. His behaviour as a public man has

also been dealt with pretty fully ; and I think we may safely conclude that in neither case can the verdict be a really unfavourable one. Dryden, no doubt, was not austerely virtuous. He was not one of the men who lay down a comprehensive scheme of moral, political, and intellectual conduct, and follow out that scheme, come wind, come weather. It is probable that he was quite aware of the existence and alive to the merits of cakes and ale. He was not an economical man, and he had no scruple in filling up gaps in his income with pensions and presents. But all these things were the way of his world, and he was not excessive in following it. On the other hand, all trustworthy testimony concurs in praising his amiable and kindly disposition, his freedom from literary arrogance, and his willingness to encourage and assist youthful aspirants in literature. Mercilessly hard as he hit his antagonists, it must be remembered that he was rarely the first to strike. On the whole, putting aside his licence of language, which is absolutely inexcusable, but for which it must be remembered he not only made an ample apology, but such amends as were possible by earnestly dissuading others from following his example, we shall be safe in saying that, though he was assuredly no saint, there were not so very many better men then living than John Dryden.

A shorter summary will suffice for the literary aspect of the matter ; for Dryden's peculiarities in this respect have already been treated fully enough. In one of his own last letters he states that his life-object had been to improve the language, and especially the poetry. He had accomplished it. With our different estimate of the value of old English literature, we cannot indeed adopt Johnson's famous metaphor, and say that " he found

English of brick and left it of marble." The comparison
of *Hamlet* and *Macbeth* to " brick," with *Don Sebastian*
and the *Spanish Friar* for " marble," would be absurd.
But in truth the terms of the comparison are inappropriate.
English as Dryden found it—and it must be remembered
that he found it not the English of Shakespeare and
Bacon, not even the English of such survivals as Milton
and Taylor, but the English of persons like Cowley,
Davenant, and their likes—was not wholly marble or
wholly brick. No such metaphor can conveniently
describe it. It was rather an instrument or machine
which had in times past turned out splendid work, but
work comparatively limited in kind, and liable to constant
flaws and imperfections of more or less magnitude. In
the hands of the men who had lately worked it, the good
work had been far less in quantity and inferior in quality ;
the faults and flaws had been great and numerous.
Dryden so altered the instrument and its working that, at
its best, it produced a less splendid result than before,
and became less suited for some of the highest applica-
tions, but at the same time became available for a far
greater variety of ordinary purposes, was far surer in its
working, without extraordinary genius on the part of the
worker, and was almost secure against the grosser imperfections. The forty years' work which is at once the
record and the example of this accomplishment is
itself full of faults and blemishes, but they are always
committed in the effort to improve. Dryden is always
striving, and consciously striving, to find better literary
forms, a better vocabulary, better metres, better constructions, better style. He may, in no one branch, have
attained the entire and flawless perfection which distinguishes Pope as far as he goes. But the range of

Dryden is to the range of Pope as that of a forest to a shrubbery, and in this case priority is everything, and the priority is on the side of Dryden. He is not our greatest poet; far from it. But there is one point in which the superlative may safely be applied to him. Considering what he started with, what he accomplished, and what advantages he left to his successors, he must be pronounced, without exception, the greatest craftsman in English letters, and as such he ought to be regarded with peculiar veneration by all who, in however humble a capacity, are connected with the craft.

This general estimate, as well as much of the detailed criticism on which it is based, and which will be found in the preceding chapters, will no doubt seem exaggerated to not a few persons, to the judgment of some at least of whom I should be sorry that it should seem so. The truth is, that while the criticism of poetry is in such a disorderly state as it is at present in regard to general principles, it cannot be expected that there should be any agreement between individual practitioners of it on individual points. So long as any one holds a definition of poetry which regards it wholly or chiefly from the point of view of its subject-matter, wide differences are unavoidable. But if we hold what I venture to think the only Catholic faith with regard to it, that it consists not in a selection of subjects, but in a method of treatment, then it seems to me that all difficulty vanishes. We get out of the hopeless and sterile controversies as to whether Shelley was a greater poet than Dryden, or Dryden a greater poet than Shelley. For my part, I yield to no man living in rational admiration for either, but I decline altogether to assign marks to each in a competitive examination. There are, as it seems to me, many mansions in poetry, and the great poets live apart in them. What constitutes a great poet is supremacy in his own line of poetical expression. Such supremacy must of course be shown in work of sufficient bulk and variety, on the principle that one swallow does not make a summer. We cannot call Lovelace a great poet, or Barnabe Barnes; perhaps we cannot give the name to Collins or to Gray. We must be satisfied that the poet has his faculty of expression well at command, not merely that it sometimes visits him in a casual manner; and we must know that he can apply it in a sufficient number of different ways. But when we see that he can under these conditions exhibit pretty constantly the poetical *differentia*, the power of making the common uncommon by the use of articulate language in metrical arrangement so as to excite indefinite suggestions of beauty, then he must be acknowledged a master.

When we want to see whether a man is a great poet or not, let us take him in his commonplaces, and see what he does with them. Here are four lines which are among the last that Dryden wrote; they occur in the address to the Duchess of Ormond, who was, it must be remembered, by birth Lady Margaret Somerset :—

> O daughter of the rose, whose cheeks unite
> The differing titles of the red and white,
> Who heaven's alternate beauty well display,
> The blush of morning and the milky way.

The ideas contained in these lines are as old, beyond all doubt, as the practice of love-making between persons of the Caucasian type of physiognomy, and the images in which those ideas are expressed are in themselves as well worn as the stones of the Pyramids. But I maintain that any poetical critic worth his salt could, without knowing who wrote them, but merely from the arrangement of the words, the rhythm and cadence of the line, and the manner in which the images are presented, write "This is a poet, and probably a great poet," across them, and that he would be right in doing so. When such a critic, in reading the works of the author of these lines, finds that the same touch is, if not invariably, almost always present ; that in the handling of the most unpromising themes, the *mots rayonnants*, the *mots de lumière* are never lacking ; that the suggested images of beauty never fail for long together ; then he is justified in striking out the "probably" and writing "This is a great poet." If he tries to go further, and to range his great poets in order of merit, he will almost certainly fail. He cannot count up the beauties in one, and then the beauties in the other, and strike the balance accordingly. He can only say, "There is the faculty of producing those beauties ; it is exercised under such conditions, and with such results, that there is no doubt of its being a native and resident faculty, not a mere casual inspiration of the moment ; and this being so, I pronounce the man a poet, and a great one." This can be said of Dryden, as it can be said of Shelley, or Spenser, or Keats, to name only the great English poets who are most dissimilar to him in subject and in style. All beyond this is treacherous speculation. The critic quits the assistance of a plain and catholic theory of poetry, and developes all sorts of private judgments, and not improbably private crotchets. The ideas which this poet works on are more congenial to his ideas than the ideas which that poet works on ; the dialect of one is softer to his ear than the dialect of another ; very frequently some characteristic which has not the remotest connexion with his poetical merits or demerits makes the scale turn. Of only one poet can it be safely said that he is greater than the other great poets, for the reason that in Dryden's own words he is larger and more comprehensive than any of them.   But with the exception of Shakespeare, the greatest poets in different styles are, in the eyes of a sound poetical criticism, very much on an equality.   Dryden's peculiar gift, in which no poet of any language has surpassed him, is the faculty of treating any subject which he does treat poetically.   His range is enormous, and wherever it is deficient, it is possible to see that external circumstances had to do with the apparent limitation.   That the author of the tremendous satire of the political pieces should be the author of the exquisite lyrics scattered about the plays ; that the special pleader of *Religio Laici* should be the tale-teller of *Palamon and Arcite*, are things which, the more carefully I study other poets and their comparatively limited perfection, astonish me the more.   My natural man may like *Kubla Khan*, or the *Ode on a Grecian Urn*, or the *Ode on Intimations of Immortality*, or *O World ! O Life ! O Time !* with an intenser liking than that which it feels for anything of Dryden's.   But that arises from the pure accident that I was born in the first half of the nineteenth century, and Dryden in the first half of the seventeenth.   The whirligig of time has altered and is altering this relation between poet and reader in every generation.   But what it cannot alter is the fact that the poetical virtue which is present in Dryden is the same poetical virtue that is present in Lucretius and in Æschylus, in Shelley and in Spenser, in Heine and in Hugo.

THE END.